"May I commend to you the n   Holmes in his new book, *Fii Ministry*. This book will be an encouragement to all who read it, and it tells of lessons learned through several decades of ministry. Having known Sonny for many years, I can tell you that he has lived out what he teaches in this book. He served well and has finished well. His teaching is practical and relevant to every pastor and person who picks up this book. I commend it to you and pray that it will be the blessing to you that it was to me."

—Frank S. Page, PhD,
president and Chief Executive Officer,
SBC Executive Committee

"As a former coworker of Sonny's I had a front-row seat to observe his highly skilled shepherding of shepherds. I am so glad he has written down his insights for all of us who work with church leaders."

—Reggie McNeal,
bestselling author, *A Work of Heart: Understanding How God Shapes Spiritual Leaders*

"I have learned that wise people listen when wise people are speaking. Sonny Holmes has collected a bucket load of wisdom over his many years of successful pastoral leadership. He hasn't seen it all, but he has sure experienced a lot! Most importantly, he has been successful at whatever task God gave him. That's why leaders, especially church leaders, need to read this book. It will help you accomplish one of the most important feats of leadership: finishing well."

—Dr. Richard Blackaby,
coauthor of *Experiencing God* and *Spiritual Leadership*

"Research shows that hundreds of pastors step away from ministry each month. This figure is astounding. Sonny Holmes has a heart for those struggling in their service to the Lord who have either left ministry or are contemplating such a move. His insights come from over thirty years as a pastor and help to provide clarity to calling, encouragement, and a challenge to stay the course. *Finish. Period. Going the Distance in Ministry* is a tremendous resource for those considering ministry, struggling in ministry, or serving as a mentor or advisor to ministers."

—Dr. Tom Hellams, vice president for denominational relations, chief of staff, Office of the President, The Southern Baptist Theological Seminary, Louisville, Kentucky

"I can't remember a time when Sonny wasn't encouraging, equipping, or empowering pastors. In this insightful book, Sonny *looks back* at all God has taught him through decades of ministry in churches and in denominational work. Sonny also takes a *look around* at current issues, structures, and methodologies which cause pastors to be discouraged or even quit. Sonny's *look ahead* is practical counsel for pastors on how to stay strong, lead with humility, and work with Jesus to build His kingdom."

—Curt Bradford, retired pastor, Riverbluff Church, North Charleston, SC

"Ministry isn't for the faint of heart! Whatever you call it, coaching, mentoring, 'working with pastors,' this is a great tool, as you have those candid conversations with those who feel called into the ministry. Dr. Holmes has simply put the issues before you. Paul wrote, 'Serving the Lord with all humility, with tears, and with the trials that came to me through the plots of the Jews' (Acts 20:19). And yet some churches are possibly even worse. I have known Sonny (Dr. Holmes) for close to fifteen years and saw firsthand how he assisted pastors in South Carolina. This book will truly be of help!"

—Roger E. Orman,
Mississippi Baptist Convention staff,
team leader for the Discipleship Development Center,
Sunday school specialist

"I have heard all my ministry of the few pastors that actually finish in ministry. The low number is alarming! So grateful Sonny Holmes has allowed his burden to become action in order to address a great need. May you read this book and join the force for caring and changing."

—Johnny M. Hunt,
pastor, First Baptist, Woodstock, Georgia

"I have worked with literally hundreds of church planters and pastors, and I can't think of anyone who can speak into our calling and finishing well with more insight than Sonny Holmes. Sonny has sacrificially invested in many young leaders and passionately encouraged many pastors. His commitment to healthy leaders so that we can take the whole gospel to the whole city is reflected on every page of this book."

—Neal McGlohon,
lead visionary, The Cypress Project

"Dr. Sonny Holmes has a passion to see those who serve in the ministry not only finish but also finish well. In *Finish. Period.*, he shares practical wisdom from more than thirty-four years of ministry experience in various settings (e.g., local church, state convention). Those who are currently in the ministry and struggling with issues such as their call or conflict within the church will benefit greatly from this book. In addition, those considering full-time Christian ministry will find a realistic yet encouraging picture of what they will likely face. Dr. Holmes speaks with truth, grace and wisdom."

—Michael L. Bryant, PhD,
dean, School of Christian Studies,
Charleston Southern University,
Charleston, SC

"Sonny Holmes is a pastor's pastor. I personally have benefitted in my pastoral ministry from his wisdom and counsel, which are both biblical and practical. He understands the pressures, stresses, and joys that pastors face on a daily basis. In *Finish. Period.* Sonny offers pastors of all ages and levels of experience sound counsel and exhortation that will help them finish the race of ministry to which God has called them. He is a blessing to pastors, and this book will bless pastors who desire to stay the course and finish."

—Dr. Tim McKnight, assistant professor of Missions
and Youth Ministry, Anderson University

SONNY HOLMES

FINISH. PERIOD.

GOING THE DISTANCE IN MINISTRY

WESTBOW
PRESS®
A DIVISION OF THOMAS NELSON
& ZONDERVAN

WestBow Press books may be ordered through booksellers or by contacting:

WestBow Press
A Division of Thomas Nelson & Zondervan
1663 Liberty Drive
Bloomington, IN 47403
www.westbowpress.com
1 (866) 928-1240

ISBN: 978-1-5127-1309-1 (sc)
ISBN: 978-1-5127-1310-7 (hc)
ISBN: 978-1-5127-1308-4 (e)

Library of Congress Control Number: 2015915389

Print information available on the last page.

WestBow Press rev. date: 09/24/2015

Contents

Foreword

Sonny Holmes is a dear and trusted friend. In God's providence, I got to know him when he became a trustee at Southeastern Baptist Theological Seminary. Since then my love and admiration for him has grown year by year. He is a man of unusual insight and wisdom. He is also a man who has walked through the refiner's fire and come out on the other end with his faith intact and his love for Christ strengthened. I know few men who understand the blessings and challenges of ministry better than Sonny Holmes. The evidences of my conviction are clearly seen in *Finish. Period.* It is one thing to begin ministry well and even to do it well for a season. It is something altogether different to finish it well. This work is filled with good, godly counsel that can help those in ministry cross the finish line to hear from King Jesus, "Well done, my good and faithful servant." I was blessed, challenged, and encouraged by this book, and so I delight in commending it to others. It is my hope and prayer you will take to heart the nuggets of gold contained in these pages. You will be better equipped to serve the Lord's church and complete your God-called assignment if you do.

—Daniel L. Akin, president, Southeastern Baptist
Theological Seminary, Wake Forest, NC

Acknowledgments

She said yes. Forty-two years ago, she gave me the nod after a pretty clumsy marriage proposal. That night, my words tumbled out a mess, and she said yes anyway. She's said yes ever since then too—when the bank moved us to a new, unknown place, when I left the security of the banking world for a hospital administrative position, when we purchased our first and second houses, had children, and joined Baptist churches along the way.

Even more, she said yes when we answered His call to full-time Christian ministry, sold our house, and took two babies to Southeastern Baptist Theological Seminary. She's echoed that yes when we've moved to fulfill that call—to the "hurricane" outside of Wake Forest, North Carolina; Goose Creek, South Carolina; Greenville, South Carolina; Columbia, South Carolina; and finally, North Charleston, South Carolina. Her constant yes endured a stretch as WMU director, organist, pianist, Sunday school teacher, choir member, small-group leader, and thirty-four years as pastoral sidekick. In all, she was the positive influence over two children and a corps of good friends, and a stabilizing factor in many family times.

So to Harriet Thomas Holmes I dedicate this stuff, knowing that her worth out-values any ideas I could have. Her life of yes has blessed and resourced me constantly. When there was an occasional no, it was in her role as the "assistant Holy Spirit," the special character of a woman He used as a conduit for His truth.

Other people have been saying things too. Liz, Scott, John Lewis, and Laura, our children and grandchildren, have always been loud in the cheering section. Katherine Holmes, our sweet daughter-in-law, always has a word of encouragement and has taught me so much about overcoming adversity. The Chester (my dad) taught me to love words, read them prolifically, and write them. Perhaps more than anything, he taught us how to laugh. My sweet mother, Esther Mae Owens Holmes, taught us to believe His words and discover comfort in the expressions of hope and faith from others.

Our churches have contributed to the conversations of this journey as well. Woodland Baptist Church, our first pastorate, taught me the first words and actions of ministry. They put their names alongside mine on a certificate of ordination and allowed me to fail as I learned the many metrics of pastoral service. First Baptist Church of Goose Creek taught me the basics of leadership, the thrill of working with a church staff, and the blessings of worship. Hampton Heights Baptist Church schooled me in the terminology and practice of spiritual leadership, and helped me learn the dynamics of change. Northwood Baptist Church lived the words of mission and taught me how to adjust to a quickly changing world. They have all been partners in thirty-four years of ministry.

Along the way, colleagues and friends have enriched every experience, taught me much, and stood alongside during some really hard times. Their words have challenged and comforted me and helped me navigate the strange waters of ministry in times like these. Teresa, Jean, Reggie, Curt, Marshall, Ron, Chuck, Ron, Matt, Nick, Dawn, Chip, Mary Ellen, Miriam, Brad, and John are etched in the softest part of my heart.

Of course, there are many more.

I remember once Elizabeth came home from kindergarten with her lesson for the day. She was excited to tell me the seven most important words in the English language. They were displayed on poster paper, written in her favorite colors, adorned with flowers and curlicues: Thank you. I love you. I'm sorry.

So there they are, the best words I know for the people who have shaped this life. "Thank you. I love you, I'm sorry." You know which ones apply.

Introduction

One day a few months ago, I stumbled across a website that both intrigued and saddened me. The site was expastors.com.[1] A power question greeted visitors to the site: Why do so many pastors leave the ministry?[2] The rest of the information on this multilayered site explored that single question and provided shocking research, working through many of the answers. Now, I don't know the individuals who run this site, and I have no personal stake in it. But I found their mission compelling and the statistics behind their conclusions reasonable, if not startling. More than that, I was impressed by their sensitivity to ministers trying to determine next chapters. I've been back to their site many times since stumbling over it that day. But from that first encounter, that one question gripped me to the point that I haven't been able to shake it, try as I may. So here we are.

At a deeper level, expastors.com was encouraging. The reasons people leave the ministry in such numbers weren't all that surprising. After thirty-four years of pastoral service, with three years as director of pastoral ministries at the South Carolina Baptist Convention, most of the reasons ministers leave the ministry had been on my desk at one time or another. Reading through the expastors.com data was supercharged because names and faces scrolled across the screen in my head as I read each cause. They were ministers I had known, situations that were real. Instantly, the work of expastors.com was more than an academic exercise or hypothetical case studies for reflection and discussion. But there was an upside just below the surface of such gripping facts and truth. The encouraging part was the way each of those situations underscored God's call in the lives of those who had faced church disasters. Each one affirmed the seriousness of His call and God's continued use of people who had hit the wall of doubt and despair and actually walked away.

There were plenty of numbers too, dozens of them, perhaps hundreds. One number stood out and seemed to overshadow all the rest. The research conducted by expastors.com indicated that hundreds of pastors leave ministry every month.[3] It stunned me, this harsh fact. Further study of IntoThyWord.org, the Francis A. Schaeffer Institute of Church Leadership Development[4], Peacemaker Ministries[5], and a number of tracking organizations confirmed a similar statistic. Their consistency made the weight of their work even more acute. Their estimated departures every month just seemed outrageous.

Going deeper, that is, scrolling through pages of accompanying survey data, was numbing as well. Every page was shock-jock stuff to give our attention-deficient minds a jolt. There were many dark secrets about kingdom service not customarily publicized. But that one reality was enough to get my attention. Even now, after more study of the data and a good bit of reflection on the underlying causes, that so many pastors leave their positions every month seems incredibly high. In the shadow of that finding, though, all the other statistics slipped to the edges. That one woke me up!

The backstories were equally disturbing—church closings, moral failures, congregational abuse, compensation misconduct, conflict, leadership issues, unrealistic expectations, family wreckage, depression, and an A–Z list of cultural pressures. Being overworked and underpaid, with enormously high expectations, seems to be systemic, the new normal for pastoral or church staff service. Factoring in the pressure-cooker environment of most churches these days, and realizing there are few escape valves for ministerial types, made the actual numbers, estimated to be in the hundreds, seem more plausible. At the same time, the need for a safety net was immediately apparent as well.

The research about ministerial tenure and longevity by a number of reputable organizations varies only slightly. Each one does the background work, conducts the surveys, and reports their angles on the findings to support their specific missions. The slight variations in reporting the data may simply be the result of denominational differences, how the information is gathered, or the usual interpretation nuances defined by the objectives of the reporters. Yet even with several interpretive versions, the minimums are alarming. Underneath the numbers is reality: people abandon His call daily.

There's more. The physical, emotional, and spiritual pressures of ministry may be the central reasons for spiking family dysfunction, divorce, and even suicide among ministers. Once again, the actual numbers of these tragic realities are somewhat vague, hidden behind a cloud of shame that seeks to obscure the horror of such things. Still, we all know real-time situations where friends and colleagues have suffered the train wreck of personal and family destruction as a result of their ministry service. To know of even one is enough to rivet our attentions onto something redemptive.

And it's not just numbers and facts. The truth about ministerial tenure is also very personal. In the past three years, several pastor friends have committed suicide. The suicide deaths of high-profile ministers' children in recent years echo the pathos surrounding all these numbers. Beyond those extremes, many more have taken new directions in life. One colleague is selling used cars, several others are trying to pick up the pieces of broken marriages, and even more are dealing with the subsidiary wreckage that ministry caused in their families. There's an unverified report that South Carolina leads the nation in pastoral terminations, attempted suicides, and other shocking realities of the times. That such things are even on the grapevine is troubling. They do remind us that we all know someone struggling in ministry. It's not a distant problem but one that's close, maybe in our own homes.

My personal concern and interest in the dynamics of ministry is long-standing. It is beyond my understanding and certainly nothing I could have engineered, but somewhere in this dark heart of mine is a chamber especially attuned to fellow ministers or people struggling either with a call to ministry or in some trouble area of service. Perhaps being a late bloomer myself has given me a special portal into the mysteries of what we refer to as "the call" and the unique problems so particular to church service. In each of my four pastorates, there have been numerous individuals who have answered that call and are serving Christ today.

From another angle, my particular bent in this direction has been further validated by the number of ordained individuals who were members of these congregations but not actively serving in church positions at the time. They were social workers, hospital chaplains, college administrators, schoolteachers, or employees of nonprofit organizations. They obviously needed the loving care of a church family and the guiding heart of someone attuned to their circumstances.

Even more, when my hair achieved its current state of grayness, I noticed an increase in the time spent mentoring, coaching, or counseling fellow ministers. When I accepted the position of director of pastoral ministries for the South Carolina Baptist Convention a few years back, it wasn't a surprise to most people who knew me well. Being a pastor's pastor seemed a natural avocation, a fulfilling and much appreciated use of my limited talents. In that role for nearly three years, I was confronted daily with the harsh realities of congregational life and some ugly truths about pastoral ministry. Looking back, I can recall endless days spent huddled with a family experiencing the catastrophic weight of ministry failure. My personal learning curve was steepest in those years.

Now, as a recent retiree, there's some predictable reflection on the lessons of ministry and, more pointedly, the longevity and endurance granted me in serving four great congregations. Glancing back, I can see some things that weren't as visible as when I was moving forward at the speed of life today. Suddenly, I have realized the significance of the character building He was doing in me, the traits He was shaping or pounding into my life, and the five very clear and definitive steps that gave me impetus for church ministry over three-plus decades. These pages aren't a potion, incantation, or pill that will suddenly curb the exodus from kingdom service that marks these times. We all know there are no simple or easy answers to the many dilemmas of serving Him in such complicated and weird times. My prayer is that maybe one struggling pastor or church staff minister will read these reflections and take a second look before walking away.

The churches I pastored were never listed among the most influential in the nation. We didn't have multiple campuses or a weekly television program, and we were not featured in any of the books about turnaround churches. Each of my churches was a revitalization setting of sorts—a context requiring vision, change, and a good bit of steadfastness. All four of them were similar in that they had enormous potentials that would demand paradigm shifts of one type or another. Mostly, they were in rapidly changing communities. And you know what that means— strong leadership, long hours, constant vision casting, leader multiplication, and hard work.

Early on, He taught me two important lessons about ministry. One involved my first impressions about serving Christ in pastoral ministry. Like most of us, mine were shaped by stereotypical data and personal prejudices—you know, the stuff we all hear from time to time about working one day a week, doing Saturday night specials throughout our career, and the sweet images of a shepherd leading the sheep by the still waters into the green pastures. The pastoral profile etched in my mind was my grandfather embracing people at the door every Sunday, receiving accolades from the congregation about the morning message, performing weddings, the ordinances of the church, and praying over people. Or, just as formatively, my ideas about pastoral or church staff service were a composite of the ministers who had served in our family congregations over the years. Only later did I realize what a distorted picture that was, comprised of the highly visible snapshots of congregational life and little of the behind-the-scenes reality that is so destructive today.

Because I was more seasoned when I answered His call, I brought some business experience and service as a Sunday school teacher and deacon in local Baptist churches to my concept of church ministry. There was some familiarity with the undergrowth that surrounds church life, though the familiarity was basic. Still, the mountaintop of His call transported me to spiritual heights. The heavenly vision of serving Him for life overshadowed any of the realities learned in church leadership roles. Contentious deacons meetings, quibbling at monthly business conferences, church discipline, working the financial stress, and some of the more negative aspects of pastoral service eased into the background. Nobody showed me the stuff of expastors.com or talked about suicide and divorce rates. It was "glory hallelujah" time, going to the mountaintops with Jesus! So when a seminary professor told us this wasn't going to be a Billy Graham crusade, the personal learning curve ramped up, like fast.

The second lesson resulted from the first. The professor confronted me with truth about the pace of ministry and my personal strategies to stay on point in this new calling. Being age thirty when we decided to answer His call, I was ready to get on with it, impatient to accelerate the process and "get 'er done," as they say. With the encouragement of family and friends, we sold our house, found a place to rent in Wake Forest, and moved so that we could attend Southeastern Baptist Theological Seminary. After the move, Harriet started a new job, the children were enrolled in local daycare, and I became a full-time student. Then, by His amazing grace, we were called to the pastorate of Woodland Baptist Church. In an instant, my stereotypes of pastoral service were shattered. The ivy-covered walls of seminary withered under the grueling days and nights of study. In the same way, the luster of the church's pearly gates became dulled by busyness. Suddenly, I was a husband, father, student, and pastor. Now, I was acquainted with the preparation treadmill, 24-7 pastoral responsibilities, the reading schedule of an MDiv student, and the shuttle service for two children. Even more, Harriet and I became two ships passing in the night. It was culture shock.

One morning, I was ready to throw in the towel. That day I cut class, sought refuge on the very back pew in Binkley Chapel, and had a pity party. It was the first woe-is-me session I had convened and was somewhat uncomfortable for this eternal optimist.

I was reminded of a daily interchange between my squad sergeant and me during my knob (freshman) year at the Citadel. Every morning he would get in my face and ask, "What's the good word, Holmes?" I would reply, as instructed, "Sir, I hate this place, sir!" He would then say, "Holmes, you need to be more positive. Now what's the good word?" And my final reply would be, also as instructed, "Sir, I positively hate this place, sir!" He taught me a way to say something totally negative in a more positive way. A worthy life lesson? Perhaps. But as I called my first pity party to order, it brought an odd, perhaps perverse smile. Go figure!

Not prone to negatives, the pity party was just momentary. It only lasted a few minutes, because in that setting, He taught me a few life lessons. Right there, in less than an hour, He gave me truth for ministry: life verses, ministry verses, a passion verse, a guiding ministry hymn, and a means of understanding His call, what had instigated all of this newness in the first place. There was also comfort, instantly and later when Harriet and I worked through the list of my learning that day. At the moment though, He gave some relief. One was a simple look around. After a few minutes, I noticed several other students experiencing their own dark nights of the soul. Their misery at least let me know I wasn't alone.

So how did these revelations take place? Did the roof of the chapel roll back to reveal words scrolled across the sky? Did the hymnals and pew Bibles burst into flame, those particular texts and that hymn highlighted as burning coals? Did a voice from heaven thunder out of the sound system? No, not exactly, nothing as dramatic as a biblically scaled revelation or apocalyptic vision. Yet what happened in those few minutes was as profound as Moses at the burning bush. He gave me quiet insight into the life He was planning for us.

Someone was playing "Be Thou My Vision"[6] on the pipe organ. The music stirred me deeply, and I sought out the lyrics in the pew hymnal right in front of me. The words were compelling. As a result, I searched through Scripture for guidance and direction to enable passage through this significant crossroads. When I'd first arrived, I'd contemplated calling it quits, dropping out of seminary, returning to the safe and comfortable business world, finishing this ministry nonsense even before it had begun. As the hymn boomed into the chapel, however, three Bible verses and the words to the hymn brought some needed clarity. They have been constants in thirty-four years of pastoral service.

Life Verses

> I waited patiently for the Lord; he turned to me and heard my cry. He lifted me out of the slimy pit, out of the mud and mire; He set my feet on a rock, and gave me a firm place to stand. He put a new song in my mouth, a hymn of praise to our God. Many will see and fear and put their trust in the Lord.
>
> —Psalm 40:1–3 (NIV)

Ministry Verses

> Although I am less than the least of all God's people, this grace was given me: to preach to the Gentiles the unsearchable riches of Christ, and to make plain to everyone the administration of this mystery, which for ages past was kept hidden in God who created all things.
>
> —Ephesians 3:8–9 (NIV)

Passion Verse

> Even when I am old and gray do not forsake me, O God, till
> I declare your power to the next generation, your might to all
> who are to come.
>
> —Psalm 71:18 (NIV)

Then There's the Calling

Biblical direction wasn't the only ministry crisis I discovered
that day in the chapel. That evening, in reflection, I realized
I couldn't accurately verbalize what I interpreted to be my call
to ministry. It occurred to me that no one had ever explained
anything about or defined what it meant to hear or answer God's
call. Over the years, I had talked to a number of people, including
several pastors, and they just gave me that amen nod when I told
them about what I was interpreting to be His claim over my life.
I walked away from months of reading and questioning, basically
believing that a call is individual, very personal, and pretty much
a relative communication from God. No one questioned my
description of His call, challenged my assumptions about it, or
posed possible alternatives to what had transpired when Harriet
and I decided to prepare for ministry. Looking back, it was
somewhat bizarre. Yea, verily, He had issued a call, and I was
to answer it. One pastor even asked what I had eaten for supper
the night before, as if I was experiencing a burrito nightmare or
something.

So I tried to organize what we thought construed to be our
call from God. Notice I said "we." While we were processing
all the information and thoughts about this call, I noticed some
reticence in Harriet, not so much about the call, but more about
the timing. The one thing my pastor said to me that actually

made great sense was that if God had called me, He would call Harriet too. And that did actually happen. It had been part of our marriage journey for many years. Yet we had never gotten to the point of checking it out. So that night, after my pity party and time at the woodshed with Him, we talked about our call and sought to articulate it in such a way that we could reference it in times of ministry stress.

It was a long time ago, but I remember sensing some indication of His call during my college years. College being what it is, I had a hard time getting a handle on it, but during my sophomore year, there was an awareness, ever so slight, that He was speaking to me about my future. When I spoke to our pastor about it, he pretty much brushed it off and indicated that if God was speaking to me, I would know it, there would be no questions, and my only response would be an immediate yes. He didn't actually discourage me, but he didn't encourage me either. Still, throughout my years at the Citadel, even in some of the most rambunctious party years, there was a recurring theme of His nearness and beckoning. Someone later said it was the "hound of heaven"[7] running me down.

It persisted after college too. Soon after moving to Raleigh, North Carolina, to take a position with a large commercial bank, I joined a local church, accepted a teaching position in the children's ministry, participated in the singles' ministry, and continued to hear a still, small voice indicating that He wanted to use me for His purpose. Harriet and I met in a singles' class and participated in church at many levels. One of our first dates was to serve as wise men in the church's living nativity scene. In every involvement, there was a gnawing, persistent idea that He was guiding me toward ministry.

In the course of time, as Harriet and I continued to date, I invited her to Greenville, South Carolina, to attend a college football game, the Citadel versus Clemson. Something awesome happened while we were there, a God-thing about His call and our life together. After attending my home church on Sunday, as we prepared to drive back to Raleigh, Harriet and my mother were sitting in the backyard swing, having a parting conversation. The weekend had been their first contact, and so they were just having a get-to-know-you-better talk. Out of the blue, my mother said, "Harriet, you're going to make a wonderful pastor's wife." What a bombshell. Harriet was really taken back.

During our drive up I-85, Harriet told me about what my mother had said. It was one of those honest moments most couples must have before their relationships can move to the next level, whatever that is. At the same time, it was totally bizarre. Two things were placed on the table during that conversation that we had never discussed prior to that weekend. One, Harriet and I had never spoken the *M* word to each other. At that time, we were dating regularly but hadn't even hinted at anything more permanent than dinner and a movie or sitting together in church. Evidently, my mother saw something in us that we hadn't seen in our courtship. Mothers are like that, you know. Second, we had never discussed the topic of a calling from God or my doing anything beyond being a successful banker. Our relationship was developing, and we were certainly more than mere friends. But in those simpler days, we had not advanced to that level of intimacy. Love was blooming, no doubt. But we had never talked about future hopes and dreams, and I had certainly not discussed a possible call from God with her. It was an early discovery of TMI (too much information), and we really didn't know what to do with it.

Suddenly the air was sucked right out of the car, and we had to stumble through a few minutes of awkward conversation about things we'd never mentioned before. This was all new ground. In retrospect, it was truly brilliant timing. There were many unspoken emotions and realities about our future. We were obviously growing closer and needed a nudge to move us past that first stage of a deeper relationship. Now, forty-two years later, we're grateful for the insight and wisdom of my mother, and her boldness in getting us to a place where our future together was out in the open.

Of course, both my mother's predictions came true. Harriet and I were engaged a couple of months later, and eight years and two children later, we were enrolled in seminary, preparing for kingdom service. So defining His call involved a lot more than we at first realized, encompassing a much broader period. As we reflected over it all and tried to shape our experience into something we could relate to others, Jeremiah's call from his mother's womb, being set apart before he was born (Jeremiah 1:5) came to mind. There was an immediate awareness that His plan for my life was bigger than I had ever imagined.

Nevertheless, after praying through it for several weeks, we came up with five points definitive of our personal call from God.

1. **The Aha Moment**

   There was a moment of clarity when God affirmed, without doubt, what He had been saying to us. It came when I was asked to speak on men's Sunday in our church. When I initially stood in the pulpit that morning, the notes I had prepared on index cards fell to the floor. So I led the congregation and radio audience in prayer to give me a short moment to collect my thoughts. When I looked up and faced the people gathered in the sanctuary, I knew in that instant that this was where I was supposed to serve Him. What He had said to me for ten years was finalized and complete. Aha!

2. **Fantasy about Ministry**

    From that day forward, I began to fantasize about ministry, especially the areas of pastoral service that seemed to reflect my gifts. When Billy Graham was on TV, I visualized myself in that position, bringing a message to a congregation. Every Sunday, I repreached our pastor's message. There was a new hunger for Scripture. I wanted to know His word and teach it.

3. **The Voices around Me**

    People told me I should be serving in a pastoral role. By now, I was teaching an adult Sunday school group and doing some lay speaking to men's groups in surrounding churches. Over and over, people would ask why I was doing hospital financial administration. They said I should be preaching.

4. **Checking It Out**

    I started to ask questions about what I must do to prepare for ministry service. Soon after, I visited the seminary to determine if I could be accepted.

5. **All In**

    Harriet affirmed this supernatural sense that God was moving us to church service. In this final step, we took definite steps to answer His call.

What has this to do with nearly three hundred people leaving the ministry every month? In coaching, mentoring many of them, and conducting more than a few exit interviews, it was evident to me that many ministers could not articulate the central facts of God's call in their lives. Yes, I've heard burning bush stories, supernatural arrangement of the clouds, putting your finger down on a Bible verse, and dozens of other incredible events interpreted as His supernatural call. Whether they were real or not, I cannot judge. I know this, however. Even in my darkest hours of ministry, when I was at my lowest, when thoughts of walking away were most compelling, just being able to revisit those definitive points of His call threw truth into my path: *I could not walk away from the claim He issued over my life.* As a result, reading the guiding truth over my desk every day for thirty-four years and remembering the elements of my call has helped me go the distance.

The therapeutic effect of verbalizing one's call was obvious during my time with the South Carolina Baptist Convention. One particular incident stands out. A young pastor called and was obviously distressed. During the conversation, I asked, "Are they going to fire you?" His response was quick. "No," he said, "they're going to kill me." So we arranged to meet, pray, and talk through the situation. He wept and poured his heart out. During that meeting, I asked him to tell me about his call from God. When it was vague, I pushed for clarity. Then I asked him to write it down, point by point. Just walking through the steps, rehearsing what God had done in his life, seemed to lift his spirits. I told him to go home, pray through it some more, discuss God's call with his wife, and then tell it to the leaders of the church. The stress was lifted; they discovered deeper sources of resolve and determination. They stayed at the church for seven years and had a great ministry there.

Today, thirty-four years later, my life, ministry, and passion verses and the words to that hymn hang prominently in my office, reminders of His faithfulness in navigating what I now understand were going to be the difficult waters of serving Him in a local church. The five points of my call are inside the Bible I was using at that time and the one I'm using now. To this day, I read them every morning, that is, *every* morning. They help me refocus each day. Those four frames and that piece of paper are the baseline of every daily devotional time and the beginning point of a strategy to move forward every day.

When I left the chapel to attend my next class, the five steps and character traits that would allow me to go the distance and to stay active and prayerfully effective for nearly thirty-five years were in place. Did I ever want to walk away again? You know I did, almost every Monday morning! But then I'd read the foundational ideals, take one of the five steps I'll introduce in Chapter 3, do a gut check, finish the day, and move through another week with a renewed outlook and fresh resolve.

To organize thirty-four years of reflection and bring them forward to this new world has been an interesting process. Being an idea person helps. On the downside, I'm numbers deficient and can't support all of these ideas with statistically formative research. But communicating this stuff to an intended younger audience is an obstacle of sorts. As hip as I try to be, I'm still a sixty-five-year-old boomer. Here's my prayer: that I communicate all this effectively enough to give someone pause before he or she abandons his or her ministry.

It unfolds like this:

Chapter 1, "Finished," explores why so many ministers are done with ministry service before they've reached the beginning or the fulfillment of their callings. A certain kind of naïve idealism may be intrinsic in the people He calls to kingdom work, often blinding us to the darker realities about serving Him. What is more, we may actually do a fairly poor job of coaching prospective ministers into Christian service. Our educational preparation is first class. But speaking truth to those in preparation about service in a local church may be somewhat light. So this chapter provides some commentary and biblical support about people who are finished even before they gain traction in their kingdom service. In this regard, the word *finished* isn't complimentary. And that saddens me greatly, to know how His plan for some of us is short-circuited by an inadequate view of church service. This is especially notable today, in the postmodern world.

Chapter 2, "Finishers," puts the contemporary church under the microscope. Nobody wants to talk about it, but many congregations are "finishers," that is, the last impetus needed to push God-called people over the edge and out of church service. These congregations are uniquely skilled at destroying ministers. The list of churches with this killer instinct isn't very long or all that surprising. It is, however, devastating, because many of these aberrant, unbiblical practices are suddenly the minister-killing norm. Several hundred ministers leave church ministry each month, in part because they have not been warned about the strains of idealism so often discovered in the people He calls or taught about the realities of kingdom service. Just as real, a good number leave because so many churches are in the minister-destruction business. They eat His servants for supper. And there's a dangerous, repetitive pattern to it, a cyclical motion that disconnects many churches from the world around them.

Chapter 3, "Steps," outlines five disciplines for going the distance in ministry. Each is a definitive process articulated and modeled by Jesus. He demonstrated them to His disciples to teach them a path to the finish line, the spiritual fuel to minister long-term. These were clarified to me on the back pew of Binkley

Chapel at Southeastern Baptist Theological Seminary and have been five very basic elements in finishing thirty-four years of congregational ministry. Now in retirement, I can personally attest to the many ways the steps *down, up, back, aside,* and *away* have escorted me to the finish line of pastoral service. Learning why, when, where, and how to take those steps has been an interesting subtext of ministry. Had I not learned them early on, my particular finish may have occurred much earlier.

Chapter 4, "Distance," examines the character development that makes long-term ministry service possible. The work Jesus did in the life of Simon Peter is the central illustration of what He is attempting to accomplish in each of us. The entire landscape of the early church may have been altered substantively had Peter abandoned Christ's call before the completion of his own spiritual growth. If Peter had walked away at any of the disappointing, decisive moments in his time with Jesus, the history of the church might have included a whole new set of characters. The five steps addressed in chapter 3 are reviewed as a means of bringing the character of Christ to the rigors of ministry, evidenced in the life of Peter. Like Peter, each of us brings a background to our kingdom service—education, experience, personality traits, prejudices, family influences, career development, and more. With those, we're called to the minefield of church ministry. In the pressure cooker of every day, He is seeking to provide those character traits that can fulfill His call in us. Yes, humanity oozes from the pores of every one of us. Only the character of our Lord can see us to the finish.

Luke's orderly account poignantly chronicles Christ's determined journey to Jerusalem. Chapter 5, "Kick," defines and clarifies the endurance, steadfastness, and strength of character that enabled Jesus to finish God's redemptive work. The "kick" that gives sustaining energy for reaching the finish line may just be the intentional, determined spirit that Jesus demonstrated as He purposefully journeyed to Jerusalem. With ministry tenure continuing to track downward, and the dropout rate being on an incline, developing long-haul traits early may provide character strength to enable going the distance. In the final analysis, this "kick" enables us to resist the cultural influences that tempt us to walk away when we're discouraged, disappointed, or disillusioned. So here we learn about steadfastness, endurance, intention, and resolve. Jesus showed them to us. If following His steps is the deal, then we must learn them too.

The concluding chapter 6—"Finish. Period."—emphasizes once again the goal I had in mind when I started organizing these thoughts. It's the simple hope that one person will learn the character traits Jesus is building in each of us and implement these five steps into his or her ministry routine in order to recalibrate his or her vision to a long-haul experience. Of course, influencing well-entrenched systems is impossible in a little book like this. The exodus from ministry that motivated these thoughts is bigger than a small volume, extending across denominational lines, geographical regions, or other ministry subsets. My prayer for this project, therefore, is not such a grand scale. I pray that a few ministers will read it, incorporate the disciplines into their ministry lives, and endure the schizophrenic human roller coaster that so influences the church today. The final chapter, then, is about returning to a "one-thing" mentality, the "one thing" being to finish, period!

Then "Finish. Period." is the actual end of these thoughts. More than anything, the last chapter is a to-do list for changing the scorecard and establishing the finish as the ultimate goal of Christian service. Join me in praying that someone living on the edge of ministry service may be encouraged by a word or idea in this manuscript, and eventually continue until His work in that person is completed.

Many real-world situations are mentioned to illustrate what I believe to be important points in the thought process of this book. Each of them is an actual occurrence from thirty-four years of ministry with local churches, fellow pastors, staff ministers, and their families. Many of them occurred while I was serving as director of pastoral ministries for the South Caroline Baptist Convention. Their identities, of course, must remain confidential, as well as the names of the churches they were serving at the time. Be assured, however, that each is real, tragic, and representative of a much larger picture.

Yes, I know there's nothing new under the sun. The twelve disciples watched Jesus flesh out the character traits and five steps of chapter 3 every day. Others counted the cost and abandoned following Him, unaware of the five steps He was living right in front of them or thinking they were too costly to learn. His character and the decisive steps enabled Him to endure opposition, criticism, rejection, a dark night of the soul, and the cross for the joy set before Him. So these pages are just one old guy trying to walk in His steps, go the distance with Him, and perhaps influence someone along the way.

The title "Finish. Period." was a deliberate and calculated decision. As I prepared for retirement, I was buried under an avalanche of well wishes. Over and over, I heard the phrase "finish strong" or "finish well." So I bought a couple of books on how to map the final chapters of work, ministry, and, perhaps, life. Finally, after a good bit of reading and deliberation, I concluded most of the buzz about finishing strong or well was just culture-speak, view it-and-do-it jargon to project energy right to the finish line. Maybe it's just me, but the title seems especially appropriate for a generation of baby boomers contemplating the finish line of careers. It is even more fitting for the thousands of ministers frustrated to the point of leaving His service for something more sedate.

Our culture is speaking the language of new realities. We used to call them values, cultural norms, patterns, or customs. Today we call them paradigms. And the paradigms are shifting. Until recently, our attention was focused on eternal or long-lasting things. We were about tradition, vision, the life journey, truth, and long-term matters. With speed as the new deal, we've suddenly become a nation of quitters. Marriages, careers, commitments, friendships, and church ministry positions are most often short-term arrangements. "Until something better comes along" is clearly a default setting in many relationships. So the impetus to finish strong, with an exclamation point, has been replaced by a hope to finish with a question mark. Seeing things through to a predicted end is no longer the norm in many arenas. Now, the company man, team player, lifelong marriage partner, and even BFF are traded for more temporary commitments. Our parents attended one church for life, and now we hop to what pulls our strings, with little thought. So finishing strong is no longer the deal. Finish. Period. It's the new challenge in almost every arena of human endeavor. It's true in the ministry too.

One night, while working through the personal mechanics of a late-race kick, my mind was shifted to a commercial on television. The ADD part of me was captured by the unfolding scenario created by the creative minds in the marketing department of a highly successful non-profit. It was brilliant and timed just for me, a moment of clarity, if you will. Aha, again. It depicted city parks and recreation workers dismantling banners and markers after a citywide 5K race/walk. As they were lowering the finish line banner hanging over the street, one final, older, out-of-shape runner came around the corner. The crowds were all gone, and the streets surrounding the finish were empty except for discarded paper cups and crowd debris. The old guy was barely moving. His knees were bleeding, his T-shirt and old shoes were worn, and agony was etched on his face. When the park employees saw him, they mounted their ladders, hoisted the finish line banner back into place, and cheered him across the finish line. When he crossed the plane of the finish line, he fell to his bloody knees, looked to heaven, and smiled. It was a "finish. period." smile.

Right then I knew the title would be "Finish. Period." It was a visual confirmation of what I believe to be a necessary scorecard change if we're going to reverse the trends of church influence in America. In several ways that I'll develop later in this manuscript, the emphasis has typically been on beginnings, what happens at the starting line. We do these numbers games in many areas, and we do them well—new enrollees at colleges and seminaries, people who are answering His call, the number of church plants, those who are in orientation at missionary training centers, how many people we baptize each week, to mention only a few.

It reminds me of pictures in the *Charleston Post and Courier* every April after the Cooper River Bridge Run, the third-largest 10K event in America.[8] In 2014, there were more than thirty-one thousand participants, throngs of amateurs and professionals gathered for the annual race from Charleston, South Carolina, to Mount Pleasant, South Carolina, just across the Cooper River. Of course, race results are posted, along with hundreds of pictures of those who set new records for the various distance markers.

But there's little mention of those who finish. You see, in almost every life endeavor, we're geared to the start.

Changing the scorecard takes more than a short book by a retired boomer pastor. But as the world turns right now, I'm praying that these thoughts may just help change the scorecard for one called person who may be contemplating leaving the ministry. If there is one who will finish period, then I'm good with that.

Author's Note

Underneath the dilemmas of pastors and ministers leaving their called kingdom assignments is a societal tendency to quit. It happens in marriages, careers, friendships, churches, and every arena occupied by the human species. Tenure is short in almost every human venue. While this book is written for ministers by a retired minister, the thoughts developed here can be applied to just about every life circumstance. If you or anyone else is struggling with longevity problems, reference the Scripture passages, especially the promises He has given, to address the specifics of your circumstances.

The truth and sufficiency of Scripture is an article of faith for me. This leads me to believe that His truth is applicable in every context. Therefore, what applies to pastoral office or any other call to kingdom service applies to every other life commitment as well. When you read *Finish. Period. Going the Distance in Ministry*, you can mark out the word *ministry* and substitute *marriage, family, work, education, friendship, church membership, life*, or the word that is most appropriate for your situation.

Now, read on. Finish. Period.

Chapter 1

Finished
When It's Over before It Begins

From that moment many of His disciples turned
back and no longer followed Him.

—JOHN 6:66

Years ago, when I was on the threshold of ministry, an experienced, older mentor told me the qualifications of a gospel minister. He said we should have the mind of a scholar, the heart of a child, and the hide of a rhinoceros. In thirty-four years of pastoral ministry, I've found his assessment to be spot on. Ministry is hard.

A seminary professor voiced a similar thought. On the first day of classes, he told us, in the most serious, prophetic Old Testament voice he could muster that ministry wasn't a Billy Graham crusade. We all knew he wasn't slamming Dr. Billy Graham, perhaps America's most noted and enduring pastor. He was introducing us to real-life ministry. Looking back, it makes sense: kingdom service isn't always a mountaintop experience.

There are plenty of valleys along the way, not to mention many obstacles, discouragements, seasons of life, and Mondays.

Most of us have known individuals who finished their ministries before they actually began. Harriet and I remember several couples arriving at the seminary one day and unpacking a lifetime of stuff, only to move back home in a matter of weeks. Over the years, there've been numerous incidents of pastors, church staffers, and their families beginning new assignments but then walking away from them before even the proverbial honeymoons had begun. During my work as director of pastoral ministries for the South Carolina Baptist Convention, I worked with dozens of men and women whose ministry tracks took sudden turns or ended in abrupt fashions. Often, there was a very clear reason for such a dramatic end. Just the same, there were many times when disillusionment, disappointment, unmet expectations, or the realities of life in the ministry shifted things.

If such a large number of pastors were retiring each month, it would be reason to celebrate His faithfulness over the long stretch of ministerial tenure. To finish well is, of course, a goal of every working person, those serving in ministry too. But the research indicates a more sobering truth. Most of the pastors leaving churches, institutions, and affiliated organizations aren't retirees. They're people who are, for one reason or another, finished. Many of the ones I've talked to are done. Final! No discussion. Get me out of here. Let me do anything else besides this. So they sell cars, funeral plots, or insurance, shift to counseling mode, or feel a sudden, urgent call to church planting. It's exit stage left, as fast as possible. And it isn't behind the scenes or in whispered conversations anymore.

It makes me think there must be a missing piece in coaching people through their calls to ministry. I've been in these sessions on numerous occasions, those face-to-face and heart-to-heart prayer meetings seeking to sort through what the individual or couple interpreted to be His call. There were plenty of exit interviews too, those incredibly sad and broken moments when the husband and wife poured their hearts out as they were leaving a ministry post. Over and over again, I would get a blank look in response to the question, "What did you expect when you answered your call to Christian service or to this particular ministry setting?" Sometimes the answer would be, "I'm not sure, but I know it wasn't this!" More often, it was simply that they had never envisioned the dark underbelly of church life. In just as many situations they would confess, "I really didn't know what to expect," or, just as significant, "I expected the fruit of the Spirit and discovered the sour grapes of harsh human reality."

More often than not, these gut-wrenching meetings impressed me with the unique characters of the people He calls to ministry. Every person and case was sharply distinctive, further evidence of His creative genius. But even with such individual definition, there were usually common strains that crossed all the lines of separation, a DNA of belief that gave them eyes that wanted to see. I haven't done any research about it and so am not qualified to state unequivocal facts, but I've embraced enough broken ministers and families to know that there's something about us as a cohort that is not always factored into the calling thing.

The Truth about Ministers

There's been some research and more than a few character studies of the individuals who Jesus called to ministry. Yes, like us, those first followers were fearfully and wonderfully made, individuals to the core, as different as each of us. They were an admixture of personality types, talents and strengths, backgrounds, interests, and preferences. They all left their previous lives on the spot and forfeited everything to follow Him. That they could even envision being fishers of men is a small clue to the disposition each of them brought to His purpose. It was an exciting prospect, serving the Messiah as He ushered in the kingdom. Even a cursory glance through the Gospels reveals their shared idealism, strong faith orientation, perhaps a good bit of personal ambition, a competitive edge, and eagerness to discover a kingdom mind. They delighted Him, frustrated Him, angered Him, and drove Him to His knees; such were their simple ideas about mission. But He entrusted His mission to them with the prospect of changing the world.

So what is the truth about the people He called to follow Him? Even more, how does that truth overlay the schemata of mission two thousand years later? It's not rocket science, you know. The answers are right there in the pages of Scripture, visible in the lives, the ups and downs, and the daily grind that characterized His most intimate circle. In a sense, they were naïve about following Him. Yes, they followed Him without hesitation. In their time with Him, there was frank talk and harsh reprimand as they stumbled through even His parables, truth brought alongside His hearers in ways they could understand. That they possessed feet of clay and struggled to grasp spiritual truth is evidence of that willing spirit in earthen vessels. Their spirits seemed to be always willing, but their bodies and minds were often slow to comprehend the actual cost of being His disciples.

That those first twelve are so formative in our understanding of the kingdom is underscored by their roles in His eternal kingdom. William Barclay, in his nice portrait of the twelve apostles, *The*

Master's Men, reminds us that "the twelve foundation stones of the wall of the Holy City had inscribed upon them the names of the twelve apostles of the Lamb (Revelation 21:14)."[1] They are the baseline of understanding His call and should perhaps be our first point of discovery as we anticipate the traits of those set apart for His particular service. That we are so completely incomparable cannot be denied. To know the supernatural elements of His look into their hearts is certainly beyond our comprehension. At the same time, there are ideals, mannerisms, and perspectives shared by many believers that are evidenced in them and in us. There's something about the people He calls that must be noted.

The harsh truth is that many people today are answering what they perceive to be a call from God and are then bailing out when they discover the downsides and truth about representing Him in vocational life. There's something about ministry in a church of humans that is lethal at times. Then again, there's something about the people He calls to ministry that almost guarantees a troubling landscape for those pursuing that call. Having counseled so many of them through every conceivable ministry crisis, I have discovered the hopeful belief system that superintends ministerial attitudes. When those hopes are dashed or tarnished, the brokenness is more intense than I can relate. There's just something about the people He calls.

It's painting with a broad brush, but Matthew 4, the calling of the first disciples, is a good example of the kind of men Jesus called to follow Him. The first four of the apostles, though different from the rest in background, lifestyle, occupation, and geographical setting, are perhaps a good quick glimpse of those who have followed Him for two millennia. Here's what Matthew wrote:

> *As he was walking along the Sea of Galilee, He saw two brothers, Simon, who was called Peter, and his brother Andrew. They were*

casting a net into the sea, since they were fishermen. "Follow Me,"
He told them, "and I will make you fish for people." Immediately they
left their nets and followed Him. (Matthew 4:18–20)

The preacher in me detects a few profile points for emphasis:

1. Peter and Andrew were brothers serving close to home.
2. They were business partners. Note: the legal and accounting people tell us that family partnerships are among the most difficult to sustain.
3. They were working together.
4. They followed Jesus without asking a single question or making a single comment.
5. Their responses to Him were immediate.

Underneath these obvious realities are a few presumptions: Peter and Andrew clearly understood loyalty, teamwork, industry, and decision-making. They were brothers and knew the dynamics and pecking order of brothers doing business together. That they followed immediately, without hesitation, questions, or further definition is more a sign of Jesus's commanding presence than their spiritual depths. Still, they eagerly jumped at the chance to fish for men, even without explanation. There was a simple, trusting belief evident in the way they walked away to join Him. Perhaps it was some of the messianic fervor of the first century, but these men went with Him without hesitation.

Do Peter and Andrew set the bar for ideal candidates for Christian service? Who's to say? But there are character traits evident in them that may actually caricature those He chooses to represent Him in kingdom service.

So let's look to the next encounter and make note of a few of the same themes.

Going on from there, He saw two other brothers, James, the son of Zebedee, and his brother John. They were in a boat with Zebedee their father, mending their nets, and He called them. Immediately, they left the boat and their father and followed Him. (Matthew 4:21–22)

Once again, there's a bullet list of action:

1. James and John were also brothers, accustomed to working and living together.
2. They were mending nets with their father, indicating familial connections and a recognition of generational hierarchy.
3. Jesus's call to them is not specified, but they went with Him anyway.
4. When they walked away, they left the boat, their family business, and their father.
5. Like Peter and Andrew, they responded immediately.

There are several hints about the characters of James and John as well. They were in a boat and were evidently skilled as sailors, as well as knowing the ins and outs of fishing. Mending their nets may be an indication of having caught large fish in the deep water, a more fearsome possibility than shore fishing. Jesus's invitation was unspecified, and they didn't say anything in response to Him. Just the same, they walked away from their life work and from their father, an immediate turning from their heritage, without question. Perhaps it's just the economy of Matthew's words, but I detect here an almost childlike eagerness to go with Jesus. No argument, debate, or words from either of them or from their father. In an instant, without golden parachutes, transfer of ownership agreements, or codicils to their father's inheritance plan, they followed Jesus.

A few years ago, a colleague at the South Carolina Baptist Convention introduced me to a young man who was interviewing for a youth pastor position. With seminary graduation approaching, he was ecstatic and grateful to be considered for the position. My friend thought he needed some guidance in working through the committee process. As a result, I peppered him with questions—easy ones. His answers left me wondering. He had not met the pastor, discussed salary arrangements, job expectations, or timetables. The search committee had reviewed his resume, asked him questions about his doctrine, his philosophy of youth ministry, his ability to work with the youth committee, how his wife would support his ministry, and all the necessaries in closing the deal. He had only asked them one thing: When could he start? He was so overwhelmed by the possibility of serving Christ in a local church he didn't ask anything. Say yes, and trust Jesus for the details. It was an innocence that I immediately wanted to applaud and scold. It reminded me of Peter and Andrew, and James and John. Going with, learning from, and serving the Messiah was heady stuff.

Perhaps we should attribute the silence of Christ's first four disciples to the mystery of His call. Think about it. This was Jesus, God the Son, the Son of Man, Matthew's Messiah, extending an invitation to mere mortals. As in the case of Old Testament leaders who experienced the majestic special revelation of a call from God, Peter, Andrew, James, and John may have been so amazed by an encounter with Immanuel that words, questions, remarks, or clarifications were not necessary. What is more, we value instant obedience as a trait of discipleship more than most others. He spoke to them, and they responded posthaste. It is the model we're supposed to follow as we answer Christ's call to service. Right?

Still, throughout their time with Him, there were evidences of their reluctance to grasp what it means to follow and serve Him. What was the deal here? Were they slow learners? Perhaps they were so spiritually immature the truth of His lessons flew right over them. They may have been idealistic, hopeful kingdom giants so attuned to the norms of the kingdom they were disconnected from the vagaries of human nature, innocent to the dangers of spiritual leadership in such a messianic age. Whatever their situations, from that time forward, He constantly placed the tough demands of the kingdom in front of them. Over and over, He reminded them of the trials and difficulties of following Him. There on the beach, they were spellbound and silent under the gaze of the one who would die for them. But from then on, they learned the darker and deeper lessons of being kingdom men, spiritual leaders. He taught them about the hard stuff.

> How narrow is the gate and difficult the road that leads to life, and few find it.
>
> —Matthew 7:14

> Foxes have dens and birds of the sky have nests, but the Son of Man has no place to lay His head.
>
> —Matthew 8:20

> Why are you fearful, you of little faith?
>
> —Matthew 8:26

> The harvest is abundant, but the workers are few. Therefore, pray to the Lord of the harvest to send out workers into His harvest.
>
> —Matthew 9:37

9

> Blessed are you when people hate you, when they exclude you, insult you, and slander your name as evil because of the Son of Man.
>
> —Luke 6:22

Matthew 10 is a recitation of instructions as He dispatched the twelve on their first mission. Mostly, it is line after line of frank talk about what they should expect when they ventured beyond the safe confines of His inner circle. His counsel included clear warnings about how the world would receive them. He told them,

> If anyone will not welcome you or listen to your words, shake the dust off your feet when you leave that house or town.
>
> —Matthew 10:14

> Look, I am sending you out like sheep among wolves. Therefore be as shrewd as serpents and as harmless as doves. Because people will hand you over to sanhedrins and flog you in their synagogues, beware of them. You will even be brought before governors and kings because of Me, to bear witness to them and to the nations.
>
> —Matthew 10:16–18

> Brother will betray brother to death, and a father his child. Children will rise up against their parents and have them put to death. You will be hated by everyone because of My name.
>
> —Matthew 10:21–22

These drastic words weren't discussed or revealed to them at the times of their callings. When they'd met Him by the Sea of Galilee, the conversations were short and simple. Later, as He prepared to send them out, the tone shifted. It was reality time. There weren't any fantastic word pictures about fishing for men.

There were words of caution. Warnings were the central theme of His final teaching. He was adding layer after layer of realistic expectations over their innocent, naïve, idealistic kingdom assumptions.

In the next chapter, Matthew 11, He referenced a living legend, John the Baptist. They all stood in awe of John, the long-expected Elijah, the forerunner of the Messiah. He ate locusts and honey, wore animal skins, and wandered around in the desert. He baptized in the Jordan River and lived the ascetic life around the Essene village of Qumran. At the time of Jesus's teaching, however, John was imprisoned. As Jesus explained the prophetic office, the work of John the Baptist, and the fate of those who announced the Messiah's coming, He asked them what they had expected of John. He threw strong words at them, terms of truth about what the prophets had endured— suffering, violence, and force. He conditioned His words with a pointed shot at their idealism: "If you're willing to accept it." (Matthew 11:14), what may be in the future of this man, the first century Elijah. They wanted to venerate the prophetic legend and ignore the hard parts. In effect, Jesus was jerking them back to reality, placing the hard stuff of the kingdom right in front of them.

Of course, there's much more. Later He scolded them for arguing about who would be greatest in the kingdom. There were harsh words when they tried to keep the children away from Him. Throughout the Gospel accounts, there are verses that indicate a slowness to learn, something in them, perhaps idealism, that hindered their grasps of the hard things. One of my personal favorites was when He asked them, "Don't you understand this parable?" (Mark 4:13), or "Don't you not understand or comprehend it?" (Mark 8:17). I mean the parables were a means of communicating spiritual truth to the common people of that era, the multitudes that were always following Him. And yet the twelve, those closest to Jesus, didn't get it for a long time. Only when He became bluntly truthful about His own death did they fully understand where this mission would finish.

In Luke's gospel, there's a further glimpse of His frustration when Luke wrote, "But they did not understand this statement"(Luke 9:45). Evidently, their willingness to acknowledge the harder realities about kingdom service was a constant issue as He prepared them to change the world. You see, there's this thing about ministers. My wife calls it a set of rose-colored glasses that makes us somewhat vulnerable. In spite of our personal distinctions and sharply individual characteristics, even among the pessimists in our accountability groups, there's a heavenly hopefulness that marks our approach to most circumstances, no matter how grave.

The truthfulness of Christ's words is a smack down of sorts. Ministry is hard, and even His first followers, two thousand years ago, experienced difficulty coming to grips with it. Like the twelve, if this kind of idealism and rose-colored approach is an accurate depiction of them, we can further conclude that many ministers marginalize the hard parts and celebrate the anticipated glories. When under the gun, with expectation ratcheted high, some followers quit.

Take, for example, the key verse for this chapter, John 6:66. The occasion was our Lord's teaching about the bread of life. It's notable that there were no physical threats evident as he conducted this teaching. He didn't utilize forceful warnings or references to death in the instance where, finally, some of them exited. It was in a sedate, nonthreatening teaching time. But it was notable. He said,

> I am the living bread that came down from heaven. If anyone eats this bread he will live forever. The bread that I will give for the life of the world is my flesh?
>
> —John 6:51

It was a troubling, shocking image, Jesus, the Bread of Life. It caused the Jewish audience to argue among themselves; such was the controversial nature of His words. To comprehend eating His body and drinking His blood was a leap of faith for them. Later the early church people had to overcome rumors of cannibalism that were based on the Bread of Life discourse.

Even His closest followers struggled with the analogy, the people who sat under His teaching every single day. In response, they said,

> This teaching is hard! Who can accept it?
>
> —John 6:60

John finally summarized their response when he wrote,

> From that moment many of His disciples turned back and no longer accompanied Him.
>
> —John 6:66

What happened here saddens me for several reasons. The ironic numbering of the verse, 666, isn't one of them. These followers dropped out at the first hint of trouble. According to John, there had already been some conflict at this stage of Jesus's earthly ministry. Five of the seven signs that pace John's gospel had already taken place. At this point, the multitudes were thinking about making Him king (see John 6:15). The religious people had complained about healing on the Sabbath (John 5:7–16), and things heated up between the followers of Jesus and the Jewish old guard (John 5:18). But the teaching about the Bread of Life was the first occasion of difficulty among the disciples. This teaching was hard. As a result, many of them just walked away.

Recently I was reviewing a group of ministers' resumes. They were from all over, coming across my desk as candidates to become pastor of Northwood Baptist Church after my retirement. I noticed a familiar and unsettling pattern in several of them. They moved about every three years. What is more, I actually knew a few of them and the circumstances of their frequent moves. They were pastors who'd left their churches at the first bump in the road, after the honeymoon was over. They never stayed long enough at one place to experience His grace in guiding them through rough spots.

In his blog, Thom Rainer, president of LifeWay Resources, indicated that more than half of pastors move before the end of their fourth year of service.[2] This means that they change churches before the proverbial honeymoon period ends. The impact of such a statistic is staggering. Many of them finish before they've even started, meaning they're on the move before they actually find traction in their work. If this is in fact a pattern, it's no wonder so many of our local congregations are struggling. They're trapped in a honeymoon cycle, never experiencing the joys or routines of effective mission. They are constantly in an adjustment period, the get-to-know-you period when pastors and churches learn their way around each other.

At another level, that His disciples walked away in a moment of difficult understanding means they didn't get to see the entirety of what He wanted to teach them. I'm not sure if impatience is a basic profile bullet for ministers, but I suspect so, at least to some degree. There's always the possibility that those early disciples were already conditioned by the immediacy of the gospel or the instantaneous touch of Jesus. In the Gospels, the word *euthus*, most often translated "immediately," is used thirty-one times. His followers were used to seeing immediate healings, quick responses to His teaching, instant action as a result of His presence. His teaching about the Bread of Life wasn't one of those instant situations where the light bulbs of recognition popped in a flash. The religious people argued and debated the literal connotations of such a reference. Some of His disciples, however, walked away in the shadow of a hard thought and missed many of the greatest lessons of His earthly ministry.

The truth about ministers isn't so difficult. We've often got stars in our eyes. It's true; we're not infallible, and we are subject to emotional highs and lows like everyone else. We know "Now we have this treasure in clay jars so that this extraordinary power may be from God and not from us" (2 Corinthians 4:7). We can quote all the verses about being in the world and not of it. Our humanity means there are limits to our physical endurances and to our abilities to grasp some concepts and ideals, and we all possess the human default setting that makes us self-absorbed. Our elation at being called to His service and the ideals of the kingdom often makes us overlook the fine print, the tough stuff that what we are called to do is hard. As a result, at least in part, the dropout rate is escalating.

An older pastor told me more than thirty years ago not to become so heavenly that I'm no earthly good. Well, the theology of such a statement troubles me to some degree, genuinely wishing I could be a little more heavenly each day. I mean, is it even possible to be too heavenly? Or to be too much like Jesus?

Give me a break! I can't imagine why having too much Jesus in my life could ever be negative. There's a point though, and we should acknowledge it. His call is a high one. We're promised His presence and power for the assignment. It's not always on the mountaintop, however. We must operate in this real world. And that means mind and heart in the kingdom, and feet on the ground. Serving Him is not la-la land, as some reference it. It's a long, often extremely tough road. Walking away from a difficult thought or extreme test isn't evidence of His overcoming the world, it is proof that we're going to have trouble in the world. But then there's the overcoming part.

For forty-two years, Harriet has cautioned me about my rose-colored glasses. It's a joke in the family and something our church leaders have winked about behind my back for thirty-four years of pastoral ministry. It's perhaps the result of a stars-in-my-eyes belief that God can do anything and even use someone like me for kingdom service. There are times when I've thanked Him for them, the joys of seeing the best in every situation. Just the same, there are times when someone has to sit me down and tell me the facts of life. In thirty-four years of coaching, loving, and guiding fellow ministers, I've seen those same glazed, hopeful looks in so many colleagues. Would I remove them? Not a chance. Expectant, positive, hopeful, faith-filled eyes are precious in His sight

But I would offer the challenge for us to better prepare those who are answering His call. Quitting can't be the norm. Neither can it be accepted.

The Truth about You

1. Who can tell you the unvarnished truth about you? If there's no one in your intimate circle, invite someone to an accountability relationship. Ask them to tell you the truth about you.
2. Ask the assistant Holy Spirit, your wife, if you have rose-colored glasses. How can the two of you partner so you can see things as they really are?
3. Reflect on your ministry service. Is it what you thought it would be?
4. Can you articulate, with great clarity, your vision for ministry? Are you in a place where you can pursue this vision with vigor? If not, what do you intend to do?
5. Are you the leader in your church? Your home? How is that working for you?

Chapter 2

Finishers
Churches That Send People over the Edge

On this rock I will build My church. And the gates of Hades will not overpower it.

—MATTHEW 16:18

Some congregations are finishers. By this, I mean there are churches especially skilled at maneuvering ministers to the tipping point of their kingdom callings. Their histories are marked by long lines of short-term staff tenures that conclude when the ministers and their families step away from their callings for good. These churches know little about that calling or the heart of the person who's answered it. They hire pastors and church staff on a whim, eat them alive for a couple of years, and then send them packing when they're finished with them. Finishers. And that's about the nicest term I can use to describe them.

They're one of the reasons so many ministers leave the ministry every single month. Yes, there are intrinsic character issues unique to ministers that give them a somewhat distorted vision of church service. It is certainly a high calling from God Himself that drives them to walk away from previous careers, families, homes, many relationships, and some comforts to answer that call. The call to a local congregation is one of those vision experiences that blinds us minister types to the realities of life in the church. That's enough of a situation to make the exit rate high. Beyond that, however, there are churches that specialize in destroying those people God has invited to this high calling.

These churches were one of the surprises during my term as director of pastoral ministries at the South Carolina Baptist Convention. Having pastored for twenty-one years by that time, I wasn't a total novice about churches. In fact, by most accounts I would have been considered a seasoned veteran, somebody who had been there, done that. Once again, however, my take on church, leadership, mission, and administration was a product of three really great pastorates. Even though several pastor friends had endured the harsh treatment of difficult churches, the finisher congregation was something new. It didn't take very long for me to learn the truth about them. It happened very fast.

On my first day as director of pastoral ministries at the South Carolina Baptist Convention, I was asked to intercede in a finisher church mess. The call came from a concerned church member of long standing who was, after many years, tired of the way the church treated its long line of pastors. The current pastor had been there for nine months, and already a group was meeting to engineer his ouster. As was most often the case, there were no actual charges brought against him. He wasn't accused of malfeasance, immorality, financial mismanagement, or any of the long lists of picky complaints typically aimed at new pastors. She said that a faction in the church just didn't like him. They wanted him gone. She indicated there weren't many of them. But they were the controlling interest in the church.

It was about this time Reggie McNeal taught me a very important lesson about church conflict. He was leadership development team leader of the South Carolina Baptist Convention, and even though I reported directly to Executive Director Carlisle Driggers, my day-to-day ministry was through the leadership development team. So before I met with the group from my first case, he told me something significant. He said, "Never count opposition. Weigh them."

Knock me down! Only in retrospect did such advice make sense. At first it was offensive, an idea that seemed totally out of place in church. Most opposition in church is numerically transmitted, as in "Let me tell you what people are saying," or "I'm speaking for a number of other people who want to remain anonymous." Being governed by majority congregational vote reinforces our predilection for counting. As a result, most pastors and church leaders are attuned to congregational mathematics.

Reggie's remark took me to another place. Well, duh? It's not such a great mystery. Anybody that's ever been in church leadership knows that some people in the congregation weigh more than others weigh—and not in reference to their physical characteristics. It's one of the hallmarks of finisher churches, the way some members and families drive the mechanics of church life. They dominate important committees, have the ear of the actual decision-makers, run the informal communication systems, and often actually decide what matters make it to the floor. As a warning, Reggie was reminding me, a novice in church conflict intervention, to exercise wisdom in providing counsel. It was good advice, like the title of his best-selling book, *Get a Life*.[1]

The pastor of the church was gracious, humble, and appreciative when I called him. We scheduled a time to meet. So I drove to his rural location, where we talked and prayed for a couple of hours. Middle-aged, he was thoughtful and hopeful, though visibly puzzled. He couldn't remember an occasion of offending anyone and knew of no specific complaints about his ministry, preaching, or service. Later in the day, after we had explored the ins and outs of his time at the church, we met with the deacon chair. He also displayed a meek, servant spirit and seemed to appreciate the dilemma faced by the pastor. His discomfort with our being there was noticeable though. He seemed very reluctant to address the issues of the church's finisher history and reputation.

After lunch, during the afternoon discussion, I asked them the one question that usually steered these discussions into another direction. I asked if the decision-maker was in the room. Their reactions answered the question without a moment of hesitation. The eye contact and body language that passed between them let me know we were in another minefield. In an instant I knew that neither of them was the de facto leader of the congregation. They were obviously reluctant to admit it, but they were not the heavyweights of the church.

After a pregnant pause, I asked the deacon chair to arrange a meeting with the person operating things from his or her remote command post. As a result, the deacon chair called a lady in the church, and we visited her. That afternoon I learned what the pastor and deacon chair already knew: She was the matriarch of the church, the informal leader. She had directed the behind-the-scenes smear campaigns and dissension that had finished the career of a long list of God-called men. My learning curve ramped up substantially that day. He was gone in a matter of months in spite of my intervention.

More often than not, the finisher church moves in a repetitive cycle. This destructive motion continues for many reasons. Most significant, though, this system of informal leadership is often hereditary. One generation of congregational hierarchy passes their control to the next, and the people outside of the family circle are afraid to confront them. Regardless, it's a deadly pattern for several reasons.

First, finisher churches hurt people. At the center of this wide circle are the pastor and his family. As hard as they sometimes try, congregants seldom can comprehend the mystery of God's call, the supernatural elements of pastoral ministry, and the deep belief system that customarily superintends the pastor's responding to that call. In the case of God-called families, service in a local congregation is not a job or even a career. No, it is a calling from God. When there's trouble or perceived failure, there's a deep sense of having failed God, a weight few outside the pastoral ministry can comprehend. This injury often results in the end of that calling, the spiritual death of that dream. As a result, finisher churches become pastor killers. And the pastor and his family are often the ones crushed as the weight of trouble falls.

Injured church members live on the edges of this painful cycle. Constant pastoral rotation creates insecurity and confusion within the body. Mission objectives are subsumed in the transition mechanics that regulate such churches. If the church is actually a body, as detailed in 1 Corinthians 12, and each part of the body has a specified function, there's dysfunction when they cannot operate according to their intended assignments. They're useless and injured. This kind of congregational abuse may account for the church hopping so prevalent in church culture today. Just as much, these informal networks may explain the disinterested detachment experienced by so many church members who have been thrown to the curb by the dominant controlling interests.

Over and over, during my short service at the South Carolina Baptist Convention, I was asked to preach in finisher churches. They typically wanted someone from the state convention office to fix their church dysfunction without actually defining or addressing the problem. Almost every Sunday I would stand in front of these deeply hurting, grieving people to interject His word into their circumstances. They were usually going through the motions, with little joy visible in their worship, fellowship, or study. The ugliness of contentious business meetings, congregational votes, charges, and disobedience to Scripture had drained them of the expectant blessings of mission. They saddened me every time. And the times were more the rule than the exception.

Second, the finisher-church pattern impedes the mission of the church. Most studies affirm the correlation between pastor/staff tenure to the mission of the church. In his article, "The Dangerous Third Year of Pastoral Tenure," author Thom Rainer, president of LifeWay Christian Resources, writes, "Longer tenure is needed for church health."[2] Further in the article, Rainer affirms research that average tenure in Southern Baptist churches is 3.6 years. This means that the church is always in a transitional adjustment period and the pastor never becomes fully functional. In these unhealthy churches, the mission becomes internalized as they are constantly reevaluating vision and seeking mission traction.

Much of the analysis of church trends could stop right here. It makes total sense that churches with high pastoral and church staff turnover are in a constant state of adjustment, resulting in low-impact missions. As church leaders strategize about reversing declines and bolstering plateaus, reducing minister turnover seems a more critical point of emphasis. It's a sticky surface, however, influencing local churches. They're an independent lot. Breaking the destructive patterns of entrenched congregations is a work best accomplished by long-tenured leaders.

And that's another problem. So let me tiptoe here. Institutional hierarchy is seldom positioned to hold local churches accountable for their treatment of pastors and church staff. Associational and state convention leaders, usually on missions to serve churches, are prone to stand with the church leadership in a pastor/staff member dispute. Sometimes it's warranted by the abhorrent behavior of the staff member, a sin of enormous magnitude requiring dismissal, or ministry malfeasance that fractures the fellowship and mission of the church. In many instances, however, it's just economics. The association or the state convention cannot absorb the loss of a congregation in its giving program. With cooperative gifts at both levels on the decline, risking alienation of a local church is economically destructive.

During my time with the South Carolina Baptist Convention, there was an entire leadership development team with the responsibility of assisting, teaching, training, and encouraging pastors and church staff. Baptist Hospitals of South Carolina provided counseling services, the Joshua Project trained young leaders, JumpStart Your Ministry oriented new pastors/staff to the details of serving a church in South Carolina, and Shepherding the Shepherd and Shepherding the Staff conferences were conducted several times a year to encourage and challenge those men and women called to His service. My role was to stand with the pastor or staff member when friction happened. In many instances, my responsibility involved confronting poor performance, moral misconduct, or grievous sin. In several circumstances, I mediated conflict and engineered exit strategies for pastors and staff when there was no redemptive plan available. But in every instance, at least until the facts of a study were more fully known, I was aligned with the pastors or staff members and their families.

Budget reductions and mission shift at associational and state convention offices eventually ended much of this strategic work. Now, pastors and church staff are pretty much on their own, encouraged to meet regularly in small accountability groups to pray, bleed together, and serve one another. It's another of those paradigm shifts that has trended the exit lines downward. In the current environment, groups beyond denominational influence, like expastors.com[3], for example, provide spiritual counsel, career assessments and adjustments, and hope to pastors and staff experiencing work-related crises. This is all to conclude that mission confusion is one of the horrid results of declining tenure. A great starting place in reversing declines and plateaus may just be getting honest and accountable with constituent churches exhibiting the patterns of finishers.

Third, finisher churches violate Scripture. The relationship between a pastor and his congregation is a delicate one for sure. Right from the beginning of the search process, this waltz moves in odd and often disparate directions. The wish list of pastors and churches in the weird negotiation that typifies a call to a local Baptist church is similar in content but diverse in priority. The church wants a shepherd, preacher, teacher, entertainer, facilitator, wedding officiator, "funeralizer," chaplain to the volunteer fire department, and property manager, among other perceived needs. The pastor wants to be a spiritual leader, vision caster, mission facilitator, preacher, teacher, counselor, and before all of that, husband, father, and man. Unless these expectations converge in the interview phases of this process, they become the grounds of dysfunction in what Scripture views as a sacred relationship.

The congregation knows, at least in a theoretical manner, they are not to "touch My anointed one or harm My prophets" (1 Chronicles 16:22). Whether in or out of context, this verse does at least fast-forward us to many other great passages about congregational responsibility in the care of their pastors, staffs, and their families. Throughout the Old and New Testaments, there are numerous texts detailing the treatment of spiritual leaders, the submission to pastoral leadership, the authority of those called by God, and the delicate balance that exists in the many church roles. Yet Scripture is seldom totally authoritative when trouble looms.

In the same way, Scripture is just as clear about the roles of spiritual leaders. I usually recommend *Spiritual Leadership* by Henry and Richard Blackaby[4] as a refresher course in the character traits and mission of spiritual leaders. The short tenure pattern has reinforced a strong need for research and scholarship in comprehending the many leadership roles of those entrusted with congregational leadership, pastors and church staff ministers alike. The Blackaby book builds a strong biblical base for understanding these roles in their usually direct, clearly stated way.

From either direction, congregation or pastor, the biblical norms create a precious, heaven-directed partnership that mediates His direction through the Spirit to the church and to spiritual leaders. This relationship isn't always long term. In fact, Scripture doesn't specify term limits. But mission is central from both angles. If this short-term tenure thing impedes mission, it is unbiblical. God's plan for mission, revealed in Scripture, provides strong guidance to ensure healthy relationships among church leaders. Finisher churches violate the letter and the spirit of Biblical directives.

Fourth, the constant leadership movement of finisher churches presents an unhealthy witness to local communities. While there are many evidences of this, one particular situation is revisited every time I travel through a familiar, fast-growing suburban community. Once again, it's a church I visited during my service at the South Carolina Baptist Convention. When originally planted, the church was in a rural setting. Over the past forty years, everything changed. Today it's one of the premier suburban sprawls of one of our state's largest cities. Then, their first facility was constructed on a two-lane US highway isolated from commercial or residential development. Today, that same small building faces a six-lane thoroughfare traveled by thousands of cars each day, surrounded for miles by Wal-Mart, Target, every imaginable fast-food outlet, three totally new public schools, city parks and athletic facilities, car dealerships, and, you know it, heavy traffic.

My visit a number of years ago was to referee a church fight over pastoral leadership. They had reflected the pattern of finisher churches their entire history, and they sought my counsel for their most recent leadership conflict. The statistical graph was pretty much a gradually declining forty-year line with several short plateaus. They had never moved significantly from their founding demographics. When they called me, they were in one of their critical low times.

More recently, close friends moved to the area and were looking for a family church. So they asked their new neighbors about attending this particular church. The neighbors told them the church was a pastor-killing church, small and provincial, with a closed spirit. They have a reputation, a forty-year reputation.

And what is worse, that reputation is street talk today. The neighbors repeat the pattern to newcomers. It's visible too. This small Baptist church, positioned on a significant commute route, surrounded by thriving, pulsating commercial and residential districts and five or six growing churches on mission, is a monument to a pastor-killing past. It's the witness of local church turned in on itself, with little impact on the community.

The Ownership Issue

It's a touchy subject these days, church ownership. Many contemporary congregations make "I l Love My Church" T-shirts available to their members and orient new members to the church in "Church Ownership" classes. From the outside, it gives the impression of poor ecclesiology, a humanly devised paradigm shift about church ownership. At first, it offended my old-geezer presuppositions about His church. Then again, after some reflection, I realized that these millennial-oriented congregations are dealing with individuals not overlaid by my sixty-five layers of Baptist life. They do successfully implant an ownership mentality to their church members, a buy-in to the mission, goals, and objectives of the church. They do a better job than most in reminding new congregations about the heavenly significance of church membership. To "own" the mission is an admirable step.

Ownership in finisher churches is much more subtle. These congregations affirm Christ's ownership of the church. Their governing documents, church covenant, and statement of faith usually cite Scripture references of submission to Christ, the one who purchased His church for a price. Church ownership, then, isn't a doctrinal issue for them. It's a practical matter, and a disconnect exists between the belief system of the church and their operating schema. Even though they publically acknowledge Christ's ownership of the church, they are the proprietors who decide what the church is doing and why.

It's not new either, this ownership problem. For generations, patriarchs, matriarchs, families, community chieftains, and charismatic egos have hijacked Christ's church by claiming some special entitlement of control. Now, there are two words I'll examine in some depth later, entitlement and control. For now, let's conclude that finisher churches operate under extra-biblical administrative guidelines because someone in the church has co-opted the functions of spiritual leadership. Underneath is an ownership struggle. Whose church is it anyway?

What we have here is a chicken-and-egg thing to some degree. Is the pastoral merry-go-round a cause or effect of ownership confusion? Do congregants presume spiritual leadership because of the short tenure patterns? Or is the destructive pattern of staff turnover a result of pastors/ministers not being able to exercise their important calling as spiritual leaders because someone in the church has claimed ownership?

In my mind, it's both/and, depending on the circumstances. From one angle, I have met and interviewed congregants who viewed called ministers as hired hands, here today, gone tomorrow short-timers who cannot provide continuity in leading the church. As a result, self-proclaimed leaders rise to the occasion, assume the spiritual ownership of the church, and lock the pastor out of decision-making processes. It is just one of the ownership tools used to justify the bullies who run things.

From another perspective, pastor/ministers won't always function best under a situation where they're not central to church leadership. In that kind of environment, their pulpit authorities and direction of the church vision and mission are second to the whims of those viewed as owners or gatekeepers. Thus, there's a spiritual dilemma for the pastors/leaders. Trained for leadership, they're most often on the sidelines. And this is a tough role to play when they've been prepped to lead.

Once, Leonard Bernstein, longtime director of the New York Philharmonic Orchestra, was asked which symphony instrument was most difficult to play. His answer was classic: "Second fiddle."[5] It's just the truth about ministers again, from another angle. They want to be His conduits of leadership to the church, the recipients of His direction and guidance, the ones who cast the vision. It's that simple.

Sadly, the truth about how the church operates slips through the cracks of our normal pastor-search systems. Rarely does a search committee announce that the new pastor will be a pawn to the informal straw bosses that run the church. Just the same, most pastoral candidates will not ask questions about ownership or leadership matters. They'll tiptoe around them, wanting to make a good impression. Remember "The Truth about Ministers" from chapter 1. A certain idealism overshadows the process. What is more, in many instances, the pastor candidate is so eager to move from a horrible situation that he may not ask pertinent strategic questions about the new mission field.

There's another layer too. One situation comes to mind. The church was in the pastor-search process again. The research of their history was done, and I knew they were a finisher church. Before they finalized their call of the new pastor, I met with him, reviewed their long list of pastoral terminations, resignations, one lawsuit, and all kinds of drama against his predecessors. His response to me was another wake-up call. He said, "That was then; this is now. They haven't had me yet. I can break their cycle." The truth about pastors and ministers was evident. He thought he was invincible. He lasted about a year. It was an occasion when the truth about ministers and the truth about churches collided.

The Truth about Churches

So if the gates of Hades cannot prevail against His church, why do more than four thousand Protestant congregations close every year? That's more than seventy-five every single week. In the same vein, why are at least 80 percent of Protestant congregations experiencing flat-line or declining growth?[6] These are not merely rhetorical questions, the stuff of theology or church history classes. Such questions help define the truth about churches, one of the key elements in unraveling the puzzles about ministerial tenure. To ignore them may be the most critical mistake of the times.

It's a consideration we'd as soon overlook. That's because most Protestants, including us Baptists, are in denial about His church. Before we can deal effectively with the career question, we'd better get out of la-la land regarding the church. This means dealing with several misconceptions.

1. There's something wrong with the church. Get real. The church is the Body of Christ, among many other New Testament descriptives. Today, some church leaders act as if the Lord's concept of His Body is flawed, antiquated, outmoded, or past prime. So many of the paradigm shifts are beyond method adjustments or systems updates. A few of the more visible celebrity churches are presenting a Jesus-lite profile that draws crowds but provides little

spiritual substance. Still, there's nothing wrong with the church.

2. Younger Americans can't handle truth. Most studies indicate otherwise.[7] What the younger cohorts can't abide is duplicity, the way many congregations speak Bible truth and live cultural norms. As a result, many millennials flee congregations that quibble about business, practice prejudice, are too politically aligned, or display legalistic attitudes.

3. Only contemporary worship can reverse the trends in flagging church numbers. This again is blatantly wrong. Contemporary worship is my personal preference because it is so often fresh, vibrant, and new. It is the style of our larger service because our ministry setting is a young, multifamily and newer single-family mid-priced residential community. Many churches are situated in more traditional contexts. What is needed there is excellence and authenticity, not necessarily contemporary.

4. Dying churches are in declining areas. No, this is a fallacy too. Most of the churches that will close this year will do so in growing, thriving neighborhoods. This came home to me recently when I visited a local church on life support. Twenty-five years ago, they averaged two hundred fifty to three hundred in weekly worship attendance. When I asked the decision-maker what had happened to explain such a reversal, he said, "The community declined." I retrieved the 2010 United States Census data for their community and told him, "No sir! Your community hasn't declined. It changed." The racial makeup of the area shifted, and they decided not to reach their new neighbors.

5. Qualified pastors/church staff won't go to churches in dying areas. It's another redundancy, but it's also a faulty presumption. A few months ago, I had the privilege of corresponding with John Mark Clifton, pastor of Warnall Road Baptist Church in Kansas City, Missouri. He's leading an incredible church replanting mission that is changing the spiritual horizon in many blighted urban areas. Their high-octane, young, aggressive church staff has a passion for churches on the decline. There's another impressive note. Interns are lined up to serve in this context.[7]

So what exactly is the truth about the church? There are layers. One is that we've got to stop blaming God for the disconnect between Christ's church and contemporary culture. This was vividly illustrated to me recently when I spoke to the deacons of a church experiencing a ten-year period of decline. It was a sad conversation. In the process, one of the men said, "It's the Lord's will. It will reverse when He wills it."

Let me be quick to confess I'm no theologian. Over the years, however, I've come to know His Sovereign providence over all things. In my personal life, even through the death of our only son, I totally trust His absolute sovereignty. Yet I can hardly attribute sluggish church performance to His guidance, care, or will for Christ's church. No, the truth about the church is that we've wrested control of the church from Him. The demographics of the church today reflect our control of it and not His. Flat lines, declines, lower baptism rates, church splits, unreached people groups, and even pastor/church staff tenure are products of human mechanizations and not His. When we stop blaming Him for the condition of His body that He commissioned to change the world, we may finally be over the denial hurdle.

A second truth is a corollary to the first. Congregations must hold their leaders accountable to Scripture, church governing documents, church covenants, and statements of faith. If the mission of a local congregation is misaligned from their stated purpose, goals, or objectives, realignment must be demanded and the controllers called to account. Matthew 18 has a correct and biblically motivated strategy for restoring people who have stepped out of bounds in fulfilling agendas. Just as much, church leaders should consult conflict resolution material to assist in restoring leadership systems that may be awry. *The Peacemaker* by Ken Sande[8] is one excellent resource.

Several years ago, I assisted a congregation in confronting an informal leadership group that had seized control and governance of the church. The controllers were longtime members, all related to a local politician who liked to throw his weight around. They were a minority that others feared because they were loud. One of the younger members read Ken Sande's book and began the process of restoring church governance according to the instruction in Matthew 18. It took more than a year, but order was restored, and the church is healthy and missional today.

A third truth is that churches must reestablish biblical patterns in the ranks of church leadership. In this regard, pastoral authority must be respected. In a sidebar, if pastoral authority is questioned or demeaned, his pulpit leadership may also be softened. The pursuit of vision and mission must rest on pastoral authority, the validity of the vision given to Him by God, and His interpretation of that vision through biblical exegesis. In this regard, longer pastoral tenure may establish relationships where this kind of leadership can move the church forward rather than backward.

So, all this being said, explain why 80 percent of our churches are in reverse. There's only one answer. The majority of local congregations today are basically led by a group of controllers. These controlling interests dominate the pastor and dictate the finances, ministry organizations, worship styles, fellowship activities, outreach, and most activities. In the process, they've reshaped the church and, even more tragically, the image of the Christ who loved the church and gave Himself for her. As one writer said, they've become the potter, and He is the clay. Now, human hands have shaped Him and His church according to their will. It's an inversion of apocalyptic proportions.

There's a debris field behind this storm. It's a perfect storm, where the truth about ministers and the truth about churches converge. There's the clutter of disappointment, disillusionment, failure, broken ministers, families, dashed dreams, financial questions, callings in question, and churches without vision or mission.

Can God's called servants go the distance in a world like this one? The answer must be a resounding yes! How? Stay tuned.

The Truth about Your Church

1. Are you serving in a church right now? Pastor? Staff member?
2. Would you say your church is healthy or unhealthy?
3. Does the church have governing documents—constitution and bylaws, church covenant, statement of faith, operating procedures manuals? Does the church operate according to the standards specified in the documents?

4. Are you the leader of the church? Is the church a deacon-
    led church? Is someone else the informal leader of the
    church?
5. Did your church call you to serve or hire you? Do you
    know the difference?

Chapter 3

Steps
Disciplines for Going the Distance

For you were called to this, because Christ also suffered for you, leaving you an example, so that you should follow in His steps.

—1 PETER 2:21

The ancients said the journey of a thousand miles begins with a single step. Moderns have amended it somewhat. The journey of a thousand miles, today, begins with a trip to Starbucks. Funny. Then, people needed to jump-start the long process with a simple first motion. Perhaps that first kick would create enough momentum for a second, third, fourth, and eventual last step. Now we need a comfort moment to contemplate the road ahead. Then again, at second blush, maybe the pause to sample the coffee is just long enough for the caffeine to give us a jolt forward.

Well, these journey axioms aren't about traveling anyway. Both comments are actually problem-solving strategies, the impetus to make first moves, to set things in motion. In this regard, the question involves exploring what steps to take to go the distance in fulfilling our callings. What steps can propel us through the obstacles of going long and deep in ministry? With nearly three hundred pastors leaving the ministry each month, the way through the maze of contemporary complications seems impossible.

There's no shortage of opinions and research about the spiritual landscape in post-Christian America. The starting line for a new resolve among evangelicals has usually been more digital research, rising enrollment of eager college and seminary graduates ready to flesh out what they learned, fresh scholarship about the role of the church in culture, and a new generation of church planters ready to usher in the kingdom. It's all good stuff, fresh attitudes aimed at reconnecting His people to His world. We're all praying some of it will ignite spiritual fires in God's people.

But with the truth about ministers and the truth about churches all the postmodern pizzazz seems somewhat contrived and empty. Well, yes, we know about mission statements, branding, podcasts, websites, target lists, social media, tablet Bibles, constant-contact consciousness, marketing, and focus groups. We have team strategies, counseling centers, recovery ministries, and video clips. Digital research gives us one-, three-, and five-mile demographics and profiles of people who live five, ten, and fifteen minutes from the church. At an individual level, there are personality tests, strength assessments, life-satisfaction indexes, change-readiness audits, and capital fund-raising campaigns. Then there are the conferences and seminars, dozens of them. No, hundreds.

Still, at least 80 percent of our churches are stagnant or in full reverse. Many of them are on life support, surviving week by week. Hundreds of churches rely on permanent interim pastors who require less financial support and generally shift the church into neutral gears. What is more, scores of ministers are still leaving the ministry every month. More than fifty-nine hundred new Christian titles are published annually[1] and thousands of digitally researched articles. But baptisms or conversions remain in decline, and the "nones" continue to be our fastest growing religious preference.[2] Even more, researcher Ed Stetzer, president of LifeWay Research, predicts a continued exodus from the church as "nominal" church members become "nones."[3] It's a bleak forecast.

Going the distance in ministry, at least in my limited opinion, isn't so calculated. Jesus constantly demonstrated a heart for the entire length and breadth of His mission. There was an awareness of time as he guided them to a day in Jerusalem, a singular commitment to the Father's words, plan, and will. They watched Him deal with the opposition, threats, disbelief, and a grueling schedule. He showed them supernatural strength and a great deal of human emotion—tears of sorrow and moments of anger, frustration, and even humor. In all the distractions, bona fide ministry opportunities and personal interactions of teaching and healing, there was a finish line. He took them toward it with immense purpose and singularity of mission.

He avoided, on several occasions, events, circumstances, or complications that would have finished His mission prematurely. He was determined to finish God's redemptive plan. As He navigated the spiritually diverse and culturally complicated territory around Judea and Galilee, He modeled five practices that enabled Him to fulfill their assignment. They were on open display so the twelve men He chose could see them and subsequently go the distance.

They're steps that have enabled me to reach retirement. Not early, mind you, or because I've got a golden parachute to provide financial security ahead of the normal sources of sustenance. No, these five steps gave me the personal direction and spiritual discipline to make it to age sixty-five and complete thirty-four years of pastoral leadership. They were the simple steps I learned to take over the long haul, a very sure pathway through the highs and lows of what have been thrilling, exciting years. I discovered them early, and I have been blessed to take them when the temperature flashed up, when the circumstances got confused, or when things could have driven me to another career. There's nothing extraordinary about them, nor are they some newly discovered fast track around the harder aspects of serving Him. They're just five moves Jesus took that I copied from Him a few years ago.

Step Down: The Step of Humility

Instead, He emptied Himself by assuming the form of a slave, taking on the likeness of men.
—Philippians 2:7

Perhaps the greatest obstacle to fulfilling long-term ministry is the cult of self that so often kidnaps the identity of Christ in us. Guarded by the unholy trinity of *me, myself, and I*, the ego thing may derail more ministerial careers than any other distraction. While there are dozens of behaviors that occasion departures from ministry, prideful arrogance, conceived in a misguided heart, is so often the cause.

Self-absorption is pandemic today. Social media, large screens, podcasts, e-books, and dozens of other digital innovations have created slick, new, and highly visible platforms for egos on the make. The cult of superhero ministers is a trip wire, however. Rarely does auto-adoration go undetected.

Sooner or later, inflated egos are exposed, and the results are disastrous in most cases.

Self-denial isn't some strange, pagan, or new-age concept alien to New Testament ideals. In fact, the step down is the first human response in answering Christ's invitation. It should be obvious long before any of us experience what we refer to as "the call" to Gospel ministry. Jesus indicated as much when He said, "If anyone wants to come with Me, he must deny himself" (Luke 9:23). Self-denial is the norm of our walk with Christ. The step down isn't a secondary movement of faith that happens farther down the road of spiritual maturity. It's the first step of discipleship, an entrance to kingdom service. It's tragic that so many of us get immersed in the glitter and somehow bypass the step down. Up front, at the beginning, the step down is a sign of humility. Later in ministry, it may be the symbol of humiliation. Think about it!

Of course, many pastors and church staffers are escorted to the stage by a consumer-church culture attuned to the applause of great performances. Audio-visual and digital technology creates a star-studded runway of creative movement, hip music, and a center stage motif that glamorizes the show. It's what one observer called the Disney cruise-ship motif, high-tech wizardry, choreographed movement, lavish accouterments, and a spotlight at center stage. It's the spotlight that dims vision.

This was my most profound takeaway several years ago while serving as director of pastoral ministries for the South Carolina Baptist Convention. Consulting pastors and staffers around the state was part of the assignment, and I was involved in church struggles and ministry career movement every day. One pastor was experiencing an especially difficult time in ministry. He invited me to visit one Sunday, observe the services, and later offer some comments about the day. He really wanted to know my thoughts about his morning message.

Now, this is a minefield, a place to tread carefully. In most instances, I viewed myself as an encourager and most always took my stand with the pastor unless there were moral issues, financial malfeasance, or some specific, serious biblical charges against the pastor. In most instances, I would put my arms around the pastor's shoulder and tell him it was the best message I had ever heard.

Not so on this day. I told him it was a fine performance. His egotism glowed brightly from the moment he walked into the sanctuary till the benediction was spoken. He sat in his throne in a pompous manner, spoke in an arrogant voice, and proceeded to talk down to his church family as if they were idiots. He didn't preach. He performed. It truly saddened me. His congregation had been dazzled at first. But the shallowness of the show wore thin. He left the church and eventually the ministry. What grieved me more was that I found people like him all over the state.

Years ago, I read a stirring book titled *Escape from Church, Inc.*[4] by E. Glenn Wagner. It became an annual read because it reminded me of pastoral servanthood and the step down that usually marks the walk of great leaders. Even then, back in the '90s, the shift from pastor as servant to pastor as CEO was creating confusion in His church. Evidently, executive leadership was viewed as the new model to guide His church through the church-growth movement. Strong chief executives moved into the worship center to superintend this shift. The business model of church administration became the norm. Superstars moved into the limelight.

The step down is total submission to Christ, and demonstration of the servant mind and heart of Christ in the pursuit of kingdom mission. It is the humility of Christ.

Peter wrote about it, the imagery of Christ the servant, one of many lessons from his own personal struggles, "For you were called to this, because Christ also suffered for you, leaving you an example, so that you should follow in His steps" (1 Peter 2: 21). It is the attitude missionary Paul wrote about to the Philippians: "Make your own attitude that of Christ Jesus, who, existing in the form of God, did not consider equality with God as something to be used for His own advantage. Instead, He emptied himself by assuming the form of a slave" (Philippians 2:5–7). This same idea compelled Paul to call himself the least of all the saints and to lower his personal profile to one who had not arrived as yet.

This truth is often lost in the blur of trying to understand and explain the mystery of kenosis, the emptying of self. So do the word studies and debate, being filled by the Spirit and the processes of self-denial encompassed by the Greek concept of kenosis. Better yet, explore the term *slave* and reflect on what it means to be "bought with a price" (see 1 Corinthians 6:20; 7:23). Somehow, in the glitz of the times, we'll preach Jesus the slave and gloss it over when visualizing the model He left us for service.

Now we're talking chains, absolute obedience to the Master, and a yielded spirit. It's not about CEO, CFO, COO, or EGO. It's about Him living in us visibly, the mind and heart of a slave in the work the Master assigns. The step down is submission of our personal goals and ambitions to His, and understanding the servant model so exemplified by most of the great leaders in the Bible.

Over the years, I've conducted dozens of deacon and church staff retreats with the step down as the primary motif. Most of the time, the Bible lessons focused on word studies and accompanying verses dealing with the words *diakonos* and *doulos*, words usually translated "servant" and "slave," respectively. In the final session, the participants were asked to demonstrate their commitments to slavery to Christ by taking a length of chain and attaching it to their key rings. There was only one time when someone balked at taking the chain. It was a pastor. When he considered the concept of slavery and lowering of self that was involved in taking a piece of chain, he was broken deeply. That day he stood in front of those deacons, wept openly, and confessed an arrogant, prideful spirit. It was one of the most powerful times I've ever experienced in a local church. They all prayed, confessed, and celebrated the step down together. Later, their entire church responded to the call of slavery. He is at that church to this day, fifteen years later.

To go there releases us from the performance treadmill that marks the termination of so many ministerial careers. Living as His slave positions us to hear His directions for service and receive His provision for the work. The reward of such service is His pronouncement, "Well done, good and faithful slave" (Matthew 25:21), and not the elusive human treasures that never satisfy even our basic longings.

So let's sidebar for a moment. Most of the pastors I know are humble, underpaid servants living austere lifestyles, getting by on a promise and a prayer, never accumulating much in terms of worldly possessions. Some are under the illusions of the health-wealth heresy, faking it till they make it, living beyond their means, driving cars they can't afford, living in houses outside their small income, trapped in the lies of "much-ness." The step down means trading the artificial trappings of this pretend world for the real-life opulence of heaven's economy.

There's another troubling dimension of an elevated ego. This one destroys many pastors and church staffers, their congregations, and kingdom relationships among fellow servants. The step down, in its fullness, requires us to rejoice in the success of others while not being envious or jealous of their standings. In the mystery of His ways, some ministers achieve a standing and reputation that draws the spotlight. The heart of a step-down servant celebrates their achievements and prays that their visibilities are occasions of furthering the cause of Christ and that their hearts remain soft to Him as they serve in their visible situations. Covetousness is alien to the step-down leader.

Envy creates a root of bitterness than can distort our vision and mission. I'm always amused by the games we play to make much of ourselves and at least elevate ourselves in the eyes of others. I've known pastors who lead their rural church to change its name from Best Hope Baptist Church to First Best Hope Baptist Church or First Baptist Church of Best Hope. One day I visited a small, rural church and noted the "Reserved for Senior Pastor" parking sign in their unpaved parking lot. Or I received the business card of a friend identifying himself as "John Doe, Senior Pastor," in a one-staff-member church. Or preaching in a sixty-seat church through a $20,000 sound system. It's mostly ego stuff indicating a need to step down.

How do I make this step down? Here's some help:

1. Pray about your personal attitude. Ask Him for humility and a servant heart.

2. Enlist an accountability partner who can tell you the truth about yourself.

3. Do a word study of the Greek terms *diakonos* and *doulos*. You can consult my website, www.finishperiod.com, for a comparison chart of the two terms and how they influence your personal understanding of ministry.

4. When you've done the word study, go to Lowe's and purchase a three-link piece of chain to attach to your key fob. Let it be a reminder of your slavery to Christ.

5. Read the book *Humilitas: A Lost Key to Life, Love, and Leadership* by John Dickson.[5]

Step Up: The Step of Leadership

After Jesus was baptized, He went up immediately from the water. The heavens suddenly opened for Him, and He saw the Spirit of God descending like a dove and coming down on Him. And there came a voice from heaven: This is my beloved Son. I take delight in Him.
—Matthew 3:16–17

Up is a big word in Scripture. When God called the prophets, He usually told them to rise up. Perhaps the biblical orientation about up is just a reflection of the ancient Jewish view that their spiritual lives were a move up, as in going up to Jerusalem. While there's a geographical truth in that upward movement too, since Jerusalem is twenty-five hundred feet above sea level, it's more a spiritual metaphor, Jerusalem, the holy city of God. Since everything was aimed at Jerusalem, up was the direction of their lives.

Jesus clearly demonstrated the step up. The step down was abandonment of His own purpose, mission, and even words. The will of His Father in Heaven became His one dominant thought. He knew the fulfillment of this purpose would involve being lifted up on a cross. Throughout His teaching ministry, He sought to reorient His followers toward a heavenly vision, speaking of the kingdom of heaven when teaching economics, pursuit of treasures, life goals, obedience, relationships, and most other topics. Most of the important events in His earthly ministry occurred on mountaintops. It was the central orientation of His earthly journey, upward.

Interestingly, Jesus sat down when He taught and looked up when He prayed (see Matthew 5:1 and John 17:1, as examples). His words were always carefully chosen and spoken to demonstrate the heart of a servant, step down, and the authority of the Father, step up. What is more, there was a visible tracking of His earthly path, the real-life truth that His focus was aimed up, riveted on a kingdom agenda. He spoke about laying down His life and taking it up again, vivid imagery of the step down and the step up (see John 10:17–18). His parables were homespun stories that brought heaven's truth alongside common people, lessons that would shift their visions upward. The model prayer is His heart wish for the Father's will and the ideals of the kingdom to be as real down here on earth as in heaven. In thought and motion, He pointed up.

The step up for Christian leaders is the recognition of the high calling of Christ and acceptance of the spiritual leadership inherent in that calling. It is being a leader.

Paul wrote about it in Philippians 3:14: "I pursue as my goal the prize promised by God's heavenly call in Christ Jesus" (HCSB). The King James Version is perhaps more vivid, reading, "I press toward the mark for the prize of the high calling of God in Christ Jesus" (KJV). The Gospels and Epistles mirror the step down and the step up as essentials in answering the call of Christ. There's plenty about the life of service, being the least and last, having not arrived at the destination, and many more references of the *humilitas* step down of authentic leaders. In the next breath, however, there's more about spiritual authority, being entrusted with the life-changing gospel, speaking the very words of God, leading boldly, confronting error, and being vessels of honor for His use.

Calling is one of those mysteries sometimes obscured by our affirmation of the priesthood of believers. That everyone is a priest before God is an accurate declaration of our doctrine. Just so, we also believe that He calls some of us to be Christian pastors, deacons, elders, teachers, missionaries, or servants at some specialized designation of spiritual leadership. That God calls some of us to something beyond becoming His child is clearly delineated in Scripture. It involves a step up in responsibility, accountability, spiritual authority, visibility, and all the trappings of the office to which we are called. This call is mediated by the step down, the laying aside of self, motives, accolades, diplomas, certificates, awards, plaques, reserved parking places, and keys to the executive washroom. In all of that, missing the step up, the high calling of Christ, may be the tipping point of service.

Then there's the leadership thing, the role of leaders when the situation requires courage, when stepping up involves climbing out on a limb, speaking unpopular truth, taking a stand, or moving against the currents. Jesus stepped up when He challenged the accusers to throw the first stone, when He called the Pharisees vipers or hypocrites, when He asked His own intimates why they were so dull, or when he stood eye to eye with the tempter, and in dozens of other situations. The step up is the realization that ours is not *phobos* reluctance but *dunamis* power. It is exhibiting the moral character and spiritual courage to lead.

Now there's a bullet item for ministerial longevity and tenure. It's true! The exodus from the pastorate or ministerial staff positions is often through the split sea of leadership, weak leadership, on the one hand, and autocratic leadership, on the other. There are certainly other exit doors, like moral failure, malfeasance, poor work habits, and other administrative weaknesses. Most often, however, pulpits and offices are vacated because somebody isn't leading. That so many pastors and church leaders miss the step up may also be a reason for so many plateaued or declining congregations as well, especially when the staff turnover rate is so high.

The step up is built on several ministry basics that adjust the focus of spiritual leaders. In most cases, it is a hybrid of a servant spirit and spiritual leadership admixed into the life of His called people. Jim Collins, in his paradigm-shattering book, *Good to Great*, referred to this leader, operating in a secular business environment, as a level 5 leader[6], in short, a servant leader. It's the rage today in business, the leader with a heart.

It's difficult, and perhaps dangerous, to transition those secular ideas into the life of a local congregation. However, the step up is essential if His church is to impact a culture moving in the opposite direction. And the leader with a heart is central to the spiritual leadership necessary to guide Christ's church.

So five realities undergird this kind of spiritual leadership:

1. My calling is from God and not man.
2. My personal worth is derived from my relationship with Him and not my performance as a church practitioner.
3. My calling from God is irrevocable.

4. This calling will always position me to be at odds with the world system.
5. My scorecard as a spiritual leader is the person of Christ as revealed by Scripture.

These aren't the mandates for heavy-handed pastoral dictatorship or a hall pass for egocentric leaders to hammer others with their authority. They are the refresher course for spiritual leaders who are under fire or whose leadership is being challenged. When the going gets tough, spiritual leaders remember those five things.

Some people call it confidence, this step up, the assurance to sit in the lead chair when spiritual direction is needed. Today, stepping up is actually axiomatic, the challenge to rise above the fray and exert some form of leadership in just about every life venue—work, family, community, or church. In many cases, it's a man thing, a declaration of manhood, the machismo move for someone to step up to the plate and exert manly influence on a situation. In some segments of the corporate world, being "upped," that is, moving up on the corporate ladder, is the aim. In the dog-eat-dog business world, it's often a certain swagger visible in the chieftains of the executive suite, the bravado to lead. In church, it isn't personal power or autonomy. It is the authority of Christ authenticated in the Word.

Often, the leadership chair is the most contentious ground on the church organizational grid. The leadership of gatekeepers and informal structures often clashes with the spiritual leadership inherent in the pastoral office. Confusion over the leadership of local churches is a main cause of decline and stagnant mission. And everyone knows what happens when no ones in charge or when there are question marks hanging over the leadership issue. "Who's in charge here?" is a trouble spot for many churches.

It certainly isn't arrogance, self-absorption, heavy-handedness, or boardroom antics. The step up isn't a corporate ladder or a path to the corner office. Rather, it's just the personal acknowledgment that He has called us, claimed us for His purpose, and intends to use us for His honor and glory until He releases us for something else. It's not supposed to give me a big head or a big title or big clout. Instead, the step up gives me a big enough heart to speak for Him over the long haul.

Three frames hang above my desk. I spoke about them and their meaning in ministry in the introduction section of this book. They display my life verses (Psalm 40:1–3), my ministry verses (Ephesians 3:8–9), and my personal passion verse (Psalm 71:18). These were selected years ago while I was wrestling over the decision to leave seminary and the ministry for good. Along with a clearly written five-point outline of my personal ministry calling, they establish and define my life, ministry, and passion on the authority of God's Word. So I chose these three as best defining what I interpret to represent the three most important elements of my ministry. These verses have been with me since I entered Southeastern Baptist Theological Seminary in 1979 and accepted my first pastorate in 1980. They are centered in such a visible place for a reason. Each day starts with a simple reading of these important verses to remind me of His claim on my life, the call He issued to me for ministry service, and the specific nature of what He called me to be. They contribute to my longevity in ministry because they redirect my focus on days when I'm ready to turn in the resignation I keep in my top drawer. They are attitude adjusters of sorts, there to trigger the step up I took in 1979 when I answered His call. As a result, my devotions every day focus on those three frames and that five-point outline as daily primer in this step up.

Dr. Reggie McNeal told the staff of the South Carolina Baptist Convention, while serving as director of the leadership development team, that in church work, leadership is everything. It is true. Many churches are stalled in kingdom service because of anemic leadership or the confusing clash between the informal organizational charts and "called" church staff. Many really great men and women of God are hindered in service because they are not established as leaders. One frustrated and confused pastor told me he was the pastor of his small, rural congregation but not the leader.

This was a shocking takeaway from my three years with the South Carolina Baptist Convention: most pastors were not the leaders of their churches. In my personal opinion, without more than a passing thought of research to support it, this leadership dilemma is the primary exit door for pastors and church staff leaving the ministry.

How do I make the step up? Here are several suggestions to get there:

1. Identify your closest confidante in ministry. Ask him or her to honestly describe you as a leader. Additionally, determine with his or her counsel who in fact is the leader of your church, whether in a formal or informal leadership role. Consult *Strengths Based Leadership* by Tom Rath and Barry Conchie[7]. If you have not done so, take the Clifton strength inventory. How do your strengths inform your leadership?

2. Discover Bible verses that best describe your life, your ministry, and your passion. Pray about them, search the

Word for them, and settle on them. Then frame them over your desk, and read them every morning.

3. Read *Spiritual Leadership* by Henry and Richard Blackaby[8]. Make note of their definition of a spiritual leader and pay attention to the chapters on servant leadership.

4. If moving people on to God's agenda, the Blackaby definition of spiritual leadership[9], is an accurate description of your calling, define God's agenda.

5. How does your current context influence and reflect your calling? How do your personal Bible passages fit into your calling as a leader?

6. Read about and discuss leadership with a small group of fellow pastors. You will be encouraged to know how many pastors, church staff members, and spiritual leaders are experiencing the same leadership struggles as you.

Step Back: The Step of Perspective

Jesus stooped down and started writing on the ground with His finger. When they persisted in questioning Him, He stood up and said to them, "The one without sin among you should be the first to throw a stone at her.

—*John 8:6b–7*

The "pericope *adulterae*," that section of John's Gospel recording the incident between Jesus, the Pharisees, and the woman caught in adultery, is among the most debated texts in Scripture. For two millennia, academics and preachers have argued the placement of the narrative in John's gospel, the authenticity of the passages, the absence of the male counterpart in the sexual sin of adultery, and what Jesus wrote on the ground after charges were announced.

Set all the usual suspects aside for now. Pay attention, instead, to how Jesus handled what could have been an explosive interaction between Himself and the religious people. Most of the facts we want to know are hidden from us. In His providence, He chose not to show us everything. This text then, even with all of our guesswork and hypotheses, seems to have another focal point. For the moment, just think about the event, how John recorded it, and most notably, how Jesus met the challenges placed before Him.

Since "they asked this to trap Him in order that they might have evidence to accuse Him" (John 8:6a), John obviously intended that it be read and studied deliberately, with great care. Underneath this great text and the teaching of Jesus is a magnificent study of what Jesus did as well as what He said. Perhaps the heart of the text involves the underlying purpose that motivated the scribes and Pharisees to bring the woman to Jesus in the first place.

Their intent wasn't the charge against the woman but to find a charge against Jesus. So the unanswered questions about what happened are really secondary to what did actually take place. Eager to uncover a new wrinkle or truth, we're apt to miss the treasure right on the surface.

One of the hanging points is an obvious question: What did Jesus write or draw on the ground? Who knows? We can only speculate whether He wrote an Old Testament text, doodled in the sand, or made symbols with His fingers. Translators and interpreters through the years have constructed dozens of realistic scenarios covering a wide range of possibilities. My opinion is simpler and more basic. It isn't all that scholarly, and so I'll just float it out there for what it's worth.

Pause with me for a thought. God didn't tell us everything. Some things are hidden in the mystery of His ways (see Deuteronomy 29:29). So as we read and study His word, we must resist the temptation to fill in blanks where He intended for us to have unknowns and uncertainties. As a result, running in circles about what Jesus was writing as He bent over the sand is just counterproductive. It isn't stated or even implied. We don't need to know. Then there's the thing about adding to and taking away from Scripture. We OCD Christians with a need to know are just on a meaningless sidetrack. What He was writing isn't essential to learn the lesson He intended.

Jesus was modeling the step back. In a tense, flammable moment, fueled by the sinister intentions of the woman's accusers, Jesus was assessing the situation, measuring the heat, so to speak, gaining perspective on what was taking place around Him. His comments shifted the conversation away from Himself and from the woman. He put the issue on them, the conspirators. He took a step back.

The step back occurs when we move away from an explosive situation so we can process the scene, evaluate what is actually happening, and determine a best course of action in response to the moment. It is gaining perspective.

Christ's earthly ministry was very deliberate. In John's gospel, timing issues trace His moments of urgency and the incidents when He calculated outcomes and stepped back from a particular course of action in order to reframe a question or redirect His audience to a higher spiritual thought. He was keenly aware of opposition and the tinderbox environment that characterized His movements. As a result, Jesus often practiced the step back when He reminded others that pacing was crucial to the fulfillment of the Father's plan. More than once, He warned about the hour or the inappropriateness of the time. On several occasions, He demanded silence from His followers even when they had witnessed something worth talking about. In instance after instance, He answered a question with a question, a step-back strategy, to move the discussion away from the urgent and toward the important.

Now there's an idea! The step back enables us to differentiate between what is urgent and what is important. It's true; much of our energy and resources are sucked out of us by expediencies that burn hot right now but are of little kingdom significance. We've often joked about church splits over the choice of carpet colors or the pastor's wasted influence when he chooses to die on the wrong mountain. Learning to practice the step back gives leaders a new angle on a situation. A different vantage point may allow a whole new perspective on the topic at hand and move us from consideration of something totally insignificant to something of great value.

Years ago, a pastor friend wanted to have lunch. At lunch, he gave me the hypothetical situation that usually accompanied this kind of conversation. The pastor and the personnel committee were at odds over a personnel matter. The committee wanted to go one way with a staff member and the pastor visualized another scenario. Their differences involved a very small amount of salary. But, they were gridlocked. He said he might resign over it. I wanted him to step back and give this situation another look. My question to him was, is your ministry only worth this very small difference? Well, I thought I had given him masterful counsel. But he stood toe-to-toe with them and eventually left the church and the ministry. It was an occasion when a step back may have given him a different perspective.

Sometimes Jesus stepped back by answering questions with another question. It was a method the rabbis used to shift conversations to deeper levels. In Jesus's case, the authorities asked Him questions to entrap Him. When He asked a question in return, there was usually a pause as the questioner adjusted his answer. The people opposing Jesus were often derailed when He moved the conversation beyond their surface attempts.

Many of these situations involved His ministry on the Sabbath. Matthew 12 is a record of several Q&A sessions with the Pharisees, religious people who observed Him closely. When they challenged Him about His disciples picking and eating grain, He asked them two questions. When they confronted Him about healing a paralytic, He asked another question. Matthew tells us, "But the Pharisees went out and plotted against Him, how they might destroy Him" (Matthew 12:14). His questions made them think and often defused what could have been a climactic moment.

Then, in another step back, "He warned them not to make Him known" (Matthew 12:16). He was fulfilling His Father's plan and was aware that the timing was significant.

Jesus stepped back many times. One instance was after the feeding of five thousand men. John wrote, "Therefore, when Jesus knew that they were about to come and take Him by force to make Him king, He withdrew again to the mountain by Himself" (John 6:15). Knowing their intentions and the inflammatory nature of the times, He withdrew from the crowds to ease the tensions and give an opportunity for the situation to be redefined and redirected.

It should be noted that the step back is not avoidance. There are times when wise leaders step aside (which will be discussed in the next chapter), that is, withdraw from a situation to discern course corrections or make important decisions. It is folly to believe that most challenging situations in church can be solved without divine intervention or strong leadership. So the step back isn't a strategy to ignore a problem or shelve an issue. Rather, it is movement to gain perspective and ensure that the problem is being considered from a correct viewpoint.

Here's a good example. A friend was in a suburban setting, pastor of a small, struggling church. It was suburbia in every respect—apartment complexes, shopping areas, schools, local business, and growth. Their traditional approach to ministry had formed a disconnect to the local community. So he was going to launch a blended worship service as a first step to reconnect—you know, worship war time. He asked for advice on how to pull off this worship-style change in a basically traditional group. So I advised him to step back and reframe the issue. On the day of their first blended service, right up front, He introduced the praise band and praise team to the congregation, name by name, person by person. They were teens who had been reached through their youth ministry. He explained that, for the most part, they were students from the local high school, that their parents were not involved in any local congregation, and that God had called them to lead the new worship service. He told the church family to pay little attention to the drums and electric instruments or even to the music they played, but to thank God for the drummer and musicians. He stepped back and reframed the issue, and the church rejoiced in what could have been a hard transition.

Sometimes ministry tensions are relieved when we model Christ's ability to step back. One tense situation in my last pastorate stands out. A few years ago, we decided to sell the pews in our old chapel and install worship chairs in their place. We all pushed the idea through the mission committee, deacon body, and ministry organization leaders. But as we moved toward a decision, there was a good bit of negative talk, adverse comments, and questions. One of our staff suggested we step back to examine the decision from another angle. Many of the pews had been donated in memory or honor of church members. So rather than sell the pews, I contacted all the members named on the plaques mounted on the end of each pew. I asked if they would be willing to donate the pews to a mission church. Everyone agreed unanimously. We all rejoiced when members of the Vietnamese congregation in Greenvile, South Carolina, arrived to receive them. Hurray for the step back.

Let's make the step back an element of our leadership process. What needs to happen?

1. Get real with yourself. Ask your wife or accountability partner if you are impulsive, on an ego trip, or having personal leadership issues. Are you open to suggestions or recommendations? Or are there only two ways, yours or the highway?

2. Purchase *Strengths Finder 2.0* by Tom Rath[10] and ask each member of your staff to read the first thirty-one pages and then do the Clifton strength inventory using the website key in the envelope. Discuss your various strengths at a staff session. Find out who the deliberative or analytical person is. Before you make major decisions, let this person give you some perspective.

3. With your staff or leadership, make a list of ten things that keep your church from greater influence in your

mission setting. Prioritize them. Let everyone have a chance to weigh in on them. Make an effort to examine them from several perspectives.

4. Make a list of primary, secondary, or tertiary issues in your belief system. Which matters are open to other viewpoints, and which are not?

5. Think about how you can step back without avoiding important realities or glossing over things important to your calling.

Step Aside: The Step of Discernment

Yet He often withdrew to deserted places and prayed.

—Luke 5:16

If there's a tipping point in ministry longevity, to borrow Malcolm Gladwell's term from the product-innovation world,[11] it is in decision making. Tentative, slow-moving, cumbersome governing systems tend to inhibit decisions and create confusion, frustration, and inertia in the organization, especially among leaders. Today, most truly effective congregations operate in a trusting environment that can respond to the fast-moving world around them with efficiency and speed.

C.S. Lewis wrote, "Crying is all right in its way while it lasts. But you have to stop sooner or later, and then you still have to decide what to do."[12] And we all know it's true; the mechanics of decision making are among the most critical lessons of leadership learning. In this culture, decision-making may be the most dangerous minefield for pastors, church leaders, and staff members. Making hasty, poor, or delayed decisions may be a large contributing factor to the many dilemmas of the career grid. How many ministers do I know who feel like they can't get anything done? All too often, their frustration is about decision-making.

You see, life is lived at the speed of thought these days. Speed is the modifier of most everything we do, except, perhaps, at church. There's a business best seller titled *It's Not the Big that Eat the Small…It's the Fast that Eat the Slow*[13] that brings greater definition to a culture defined by velocity. Of course, churches, denominations, and institutions are organized around governing documents and organizational systems that keep decision-making confined and slow. Often, the inhibiters are in place because their leaders, at some point in their history, have forgotten the discipline of stepping aside. Sometimes the complicated machinery of decision making has been implemented as a protective shield against faulty systems. It's an error too, thinking that slow means deliberate. In a world like this one, slow can disconnect us from mission, fast.

Two polarities seem most obvious in the current church world. Many churches are mired in slow-moving legalese that keeps the brakes on decision-making processes. One congregation I assisted while on the staff of the South Carolina Baptist Convention is a prime example. The pastor of the church was approached by the local elementary school principal about establishing a partnership between the school and the church. By the time the church worked the proposal through their complex gears and cogs of authority and finally brought the matter to a vote of the church about a year later, the school had moved on to another denomination and congregation. The gatekeepers were relieved, and the pastor resigned in a few months for a staff position in another state.

Another congregation I knew had decided to adopt the local fire department for support and recognition. For months, they quibbled about the particulars—dates, the manner of recognition, costs, and believe it or not, whether they would permit non-Baptist fire-and-rescue personnel to participate. It all blew up at a church business meeting when the congregation tabled the motion. I thought the pastor was going to have a nervous breakdown. Never once in a long and protracted process did anyone ask what God might have wanted in his or her decision making.

Each instance, and many more like them, could have been redeemed if the leaders had stepped aside for prayer, Bible study, and spiritual discernment. Instead, they labored through formal or informal systems and approval layers that actually shifted the emphasis from the proposed mission to sidebars. Very worthy mission opportunities were obscured in clouds of confusion, argument, personal preferences, and inflammatory rhetoric. Sadly, those mission doors, in most of the situations, closed for good.

The other extreme is an emerging model. Many congregations understand the dynamics of mission in a fluid world. They are sleek, lean organizations honed for action. The committee structure is modern, layers of authority have been streamlined, and they are ready to move. In this scenario, decision-making is centralized in eldership, staff executive positions, or ministry teams. The rhythm of church life, mission, and organizational response is up-tempo. They're ready to move. Good? Yes, except when their speed becomes the defining reality. You see, procrastination isn't in the cards in sleek, fast-moving organizations. Impulsiveness is.

Several years ago, I worked with a congregation led by a church cowboy. Shooting from the hip was his style, and the church accommodated and praised the way he stepped up to decisive moments. He challenged the church to invest in the local community by establishing a child-development center. The church spent $150,000 to add outside exits to each preschool classroom. Later, the entire project was scuttled because of asbestos in the old building. Stepping aside may have prevented such a needless use of funds and a five-year detour in community connection.

The step aside is the discipline of discerning God's direction in making significant mission decisions and determining spiritual direction.

Jesus often stepped aside. One obvious example was the night before He named the twelve. Luke 6:12 provides Luke's orderly account in his usual economy of words, indicating, "During those days he went out to a mountain and spent all night in prayer to God." He didn't explore the motivations, explain the setting, or even venture a guess about what took place there. But Doctor Luke was keen to give us a glimpse of our Lord's decision-making wisdom. He stepped aside to discern the Father's will in decisive times, when important decisions affecting the future of His church were front and center.

Luke had already mentioned the Lord's practice of stepping aside. In an earlier setting, he wrote, "Yet He often withdrew to deserted places and prayed" (Luke 5:16). In the push and pull of first-century motion, Jesus was singularly fixed on doing His Father's will, speaking His Father's words, finishing His Father's work, and fulfilling His Father's redemptive plan. The forces of distraction—zealous religious fanatics, multicultural influences, a needy and overlooked population, an occupying foreign army, bigotry of every stripe, spiritual exclusivity, poverty, nationalism—all changed the landscape of mission. The man Jesus kept focus by stepping aside regularly to hear from the Father. Many references support this conclusion.

> Very early in the morning, while it was still dark, He got up, went out, and made His way to a deserted place. And He was praying there.
>
> —Mark 1:35

> After dismissing the crowds, He went up on the mountain by Himself to pray. When evening came, He was there alone.
>
> —Matthew 14:23

> During His earthly life, He offered prayers and appeals, with loud cries and tears, to the One who was able to save Him from death, and He was heard because of His reverence.
>
> —Hebrews 5:7

The garden of Gethsemane is perhaps the most visible occasion of Jesus stepping aside. Luke wrote, "When He reached the place, He told them, 'Pray that you may not enter into temptation.' Then He withdrew from them about a stone's throw, knelt down, and began to pray" (Luke 22:40–41).

Stepping back is the discipline of gaining perspective, examining stressful circumstances from another angle. Spiritual discernment is the stuff of stepping aside, the pause that refreshes our communion with Him and ensures the right track for the road ahead. The step back gives us a new perspective on a situation. The step aside gives us His perspective.

Here's a fallacy of leadership and decision-making. Stepping aside isn't about discovering our thoughts, validating our decisions, or selling our vision about mission. It's about discerning His counsel, His direction, and His wisdom to rivet us to His plan.

Henry and Richard Blackaby, writing in *Spiritual Leadership*, in their usual direct brevity, explained it like this:

"God doesn't want people to do what they think is best: He wants them to do what He knows is best, and no amount of reasoning and intellectualizing will discover that."[14]

So stepping aside isn't market studies, demographics, convenient statistics, or trends. Neither is it about weighing options, mediating differences of opinion, or being innovative. It's when we move from our agenda to His, Blackaby's basic definition of spiritual leadership. Stepping aside involves seeking His counsel when making decisions.

Up front, I confessed a weakness in scholarly study and research. My conclusions about ministry and stress are an admixture of personal experience as a pastor and several years in pastoral ministry at the state-convention level. Walking with colleagues through the multifaceted trouble spots of ministry leadership in real-time affirms the tragic results of poor decision-making and the daily pressure chamber of being at the top of the game. Learning to step aside for prayerful discernment has been a way to stay focused on the mission and hear from the One who called us to it, gives us what we need for it, and guides us daily through it.

There's an intense personal acquaintance with the need to step aside. On July 18, 2011, our lives were changed forever. Our son, Brian Eliot Holmes, age thirty-three, was murdered in downtown Charleston, South Carolina. It was during my term as president of the South Carolina Baptist Convention, so there was a lot of press and public attention. There's no way I can express the devastation of those days, a tragedy too deep to verbalize. Our faith activated autoresponses in us that guided us through those first dark days. The loss wrecked us. The stress of losing our precious child was just one visible level of trouble as the drama of his murder unfolded. City officials, court dates, an ever-present media, and being on such a public stage day in and day out were additional weights that challenged us that entire year. But that day was the most shocking experience any of us had encountered.

Suddenly, we were thrust onto a ministry platform we had never anticipated. The first hours were an emotional sea of busy-ness, what I had read in *The Morning after Death* by L.D. Johnson[15], pastor of First Baptist Church, Greenville, South Carolina, many years ago. An autopilot mechanism steered us through meetings with law enforcement personnel, local media, and all the other urgencies of the moment. My traditional role as pastor shifted somewhat as I tried to be a spiritual leader to Harriet; Brian's wife, Katherine; our daughter Liz Carpenter; her husband Scott; and our young grandson, John Lewis. Our extended family and an army of caring church members gathered to walk with us through this quagmire of conflicting emotions. There were decisions to be made, questions to be answered, statements to the press, Q&A times with police officials, and dozens of other matters suddenly thrust on all of us.

Late that first night, Harriet and I stepped aside for moments of personal grief and spiritual discernment. How could we comprehend this horrible tragedy and at the same time reflect the authenticity of our faith? Even as we prayed, just hours from learning his death, we were comforted by counsel from His Word. He gave us two Bible verses that provided us some hopeful clarity in that dark night and continue to give us direction now, four years later.

> Humble yourselves, therefore, under God's mighty hand, that He will lift you up in due time.
>
> —1 Peter 5:6, NIV

But He gives us more grace.

—James 4:6, NIV

Of course, they didn't provide instant answers to the hundred questions that gripped us right then. They did, however, give us two assurances, the promises of a "due time" when he would lift us above the heavy weights of our loss and "more grace." We're still waiting on the "due time." We do, however, discover the sufficiency of His grace every moment. That step aside with Harriet was perhaps the most definitive few minutes we've ever experienced in forty-two years of life together. We heard from Him, and His voice and counsel inserted hope into mysteries of the time. He clarified a path for us through the quagmire of grief and gave us a way to express our grief and faith. It was a definitive moment.

There have been many other times, perhaps hundreds of them, when I've needed to step aside to discern His heart about significant personal and church matters. Each occasion has given me the grace to set my own personal agenda aside so that I could discern His. It is a grace that must be practiced every single day.

So help me learn the discipline of the step aside. Here are a few directional signs for the process:

1. Develop a strong personal devotional life. Your leadership will be a reflection of the time and quality of your own spiritual journey. Go deep!

2. Listen to the assistant Holy Spirit. Go simple with me for a minute. There's nothing irreverent intended here, and it is stated from a deep-seated belief in the ministry partnership God created in my relationship with Harriet, my wife of forty-two years. She knows me better than any other human being. Her faith and personal devotional

life is stronger than my own. Her quiet, steady counsel has been a constant in my four pastorates. On many occasions, she has warned me about impulsiveness, the dangers of my own ego, and the need for discernment in ministry. You have one too. Listen to her!

3. Discover the "belief" strength in the leaders around you and involve them in the schema of your decision-making. This strength will provide a deep convictional compass to guide you through the currents of complicated issues.

4. Find a wise, spiritual mentor or accountability group to influence you when decision-making is critical to your ministry leadership.

5. Don't read too many blogs.

Step Away: The Step of Refreshment

He said to them, Come away by yourselves to a remote place and rest awhile.

—Mark 6:31

There are places, five of them. They are the locations in each of my four pastorates where I could step away for a few physical and mental health minutes or hours. There have also been times. These are the hours in every week of the past thirty-four years bracketed for time with my wife and children or simply some breathing space from the ministry treadmill. Both the places and the times are the results of advice early on in ministry to step away on occasion. I don't have any personal research to support this conclusion, but I believe thirty-four consecutive years of church ministry is the result of heeding that advice. Trusting the stats of the people who conduct that kind of study, I further believe that ministry tenure is a by-product of the step away.

The step away is the discipline of regularly walking away from ministry for renewal, refreshment, relaxation, rest, and recreation.

Years ago, my grandfather, Rev. O. F. Owens, counseled me to schedule regular times away from the rigors of ministry. He wasn't talking about a prayer closet, a chapel for devotional time, or an office for study. He was talking about a mental-health place and time where I could disconnect from ministry, decisions, and even people. His was in the garden, and like the hymn, he usually went there alone. I can still see him laboring over rows of corn, beans, tomato plants, squash, and just about everything you can purchase in the produce department of the grocery store. It was in the backyard of the parsonage at West Greenville Baptist Church. It was his therapy. He went there every day.

There are a couple of layers to my personal health plan. The foundation is simply monitoring the indicators, regularly checking the pressure gauges. Sure, each of us is different. We have varying physical and mental thresholds. One person needs this much sleep, another that. The person down the street thrives in a pressure cooker, and the other colleague shuts down when the going gets tough. One is a morning person, the other a night owl. The achiever is first in almost everything, while the intellectual is always thinking. Each of us needs to know what makes us tick and to be prepared to fuel that level of activity. Mainly, it's the discipline of self-awareness, knowing what we can do, understanding our limits, and putting in place the personal preparation so that we can function according to our designer's plans.

There have been five places of retreat when my personal indicators were off the charts. They were all places I could attain in short order, locales that were generally accessible throughout the day, with no cost, except gasoline. At Woodland Baptist Church outside of Wake Forest, North Carolina, the place was Binkley Chapel at Southeastern Baptist Theological Seminary. At First Baptist Church of Goose Creek in the suburbs of Charleston, South Carolina, it was Summerall Chapel on the campus of the Citadel, the Military College of South Carolina, my alma mater. At Hampton Heights Baptist Church in Greenville, South Carolina, it was Pretty Place, a mountain chapel literally hanging on the edge of Camp Greenville, the YMCA camp in the mountains near the North Carolina state line. While on the staff of the South Carolina Baptist Convention, it was the river walk along the Congaree River. At Northwood Baptist Church, again in the suburbs of Charleston, South Carolina, it was Summerall Chapel 2.0, a place of value in my life system adjusted by additional years of experience and need.

Very often over the years, I would put my finger on the pulse and, when indicated, slip away for some R and R at one of these places. Our church staff always knew to translate, "I'm checking out for a while," to mean where I'd be away for a few hours. It was the simplest, most fundamental element of the step away for me, a place to go for physical, emotional, and spiritual refreshment.

There also have been Fridays. That's the day I chose to be off every single week for thirty-four years. Yes, there were occasions when I would interrupt Fridays for emergencies, scheduled weddings, or other important church or family activities. But for every one of those years, Friday has been the day reserved for something off the grid.

Friends often ask why I chose Friday. It's not all that complicated and just seems to suit my temperament and lifestyle best. In the old world, many ministers opted for Mondays as the preferred day off, perhaps a recovery day from Sunday preaching and teaching, among other church activities. But that never worked for me. Monday is usually a down day for me, a mental and physical letdown after the hyped-up Sunday schedule. Excuse me for being a little egotistical about this, but I never wanted to spend my day off moping around, a physical and mental zombie. So I usually dedicate Mondays to office routine, pastoral care, and other more sedate duties. Fridays were and are sanctified for Harriet, the children, and me. (PS—it wasn't a study day either. That has always been Thursdays). To be a genuine step away, the day off should be a time without ministry duties and personal distractions.

In some years Harriet worked. So I occupied myself on Fridays. For years, I was an avid golfer, played with the same people every Friday afternoon. On other occasions, Harriet and I would hike Biltmore Estates in Asheville, North Carolina, another place on our list, or the historic district in downtown Charleston every Friday. Friday nights, we did things with Elizabeth and Brian (and their friends). When it wasn't high school sports, we went out to eat and then to Barnes & Noble. We all got a new book on Fridays.

Several years ago, Harriet returned from a pastors' wives event, troubled and broken. She related a life story of one of the pastor's wives in attendance that touched her deeply. The woman was in her early sixties. She told the group that she and her husband had not had a family vacation in thirty-three years. The financial realities of serving a smaller, rural congregation didn't include funding for time away. Providing essentials didn't leave room for any luxury. Harriet said the lady wasn't bitter or angry, just disappointed and burdened. Her husband, in her words, was wiped out—all the time.

Let the theologians explain the mystery of Christ's humanity and deity. For Him to be fully man and fully God is an article of faith that I can believe without actually comprehending. Even after reading John 1 and coming to terms with the incarnation, I am still awed by the truth that God became man and needed time for rest, relaxation, or restoration. But there it is in print.

That He invited the twelve to step away for rest clarifies the weight of His humanity. It had been a grueling few days. The locals around Nazareth were offended by His authoritative teaching. They rejected Him. As He traveled the region, teaching, He gave the twelve authority and sent them out to preach. The news of John the Baptist's beheading reached Him. When the apostles gathered to report the results of their mission, He gave them an invitation to step away. He said, "Come away by yourselves to a remote place and rest awhile" (Mark 6:31).

Here's the kicker. After preaching this passage numerous times over the past thirty-plus years, there's a new wrinkle. In this instance, He didn't send them. He invited them. He reached a personal hand out to these chosen, called ones, and He asked them to step away for physical refreshment and restoration. He knew the press of the crowds, the urgency of the mission, the stress of rejection, even the demands of the days ahead. No doubt, the toll of kingdom service was visible in them.

In response, He invited them to step away. It was an invitation they had heard, in one form or another, many times, almost a replay of "come to Me, all of you who are weary and burdened, and I will give you rest" (Matthew 11:28). On this occasion, He wasn't speaking to the multitudes, confronting the Pharisees, or touching the infirm. He was extending a caring, personal hand to the men He had chosen. It wasn't a prayer meeting or leadership seminar, lessons in homiletics or hermeneutics, or a team meeting. He invited them to step away and rest.

Ministry is fast-paced and demanding. My thirty-four years have been energized by a strength array that includes "achiever." This means I'm prone to be a workaholic. I'm usually first in the office every day, last to leave, actively pursuing my list for the day. Like most personal attributes, this is a strength that can morph into a weakness if overplayed. Most of us do that one well too, you know—overplay a thing. It's not a tendency or a habit. It's what I bring to the table, all the time.

Then, of course, there's the final step away, retirement. By the time you read this, my retirement from active church ministry will be finalized. Many friends and colleagues were surprised by this decision and asked why I had decided to take this step now. Thom Rainer and other Southern Baptist leaders have written many blogs and articles about the impending retirement of the entire boomer cohort.[4] One of the new wrinkles, perhaps particular to the boomer generation, is that many of us are retiring later. My response to their questioning is usually, "I'm retiring from the church so I can do some of the Lord's work." People in ministry smile and get it.

One friend asked if I thought He was through with me. The answer to that is emphatically no. When He's through with me, I'll be in a box or an urn. No, retirement for me is more about the church, what I bring to ministry, and what I believe to be the need for fresh eyes. OK, I'm sixty-five years old. That doesn't mean I'm a grumpy old geezer. Harriet and I are techies with Nook, iPad, iPhone, Mac, Fitbit, HSCB Bibles, and a Keurig coffee maker. We prefer contemporary music, left boxed-living long ago, and understand the constant need for personal change. Even so, my sixty-five-year-old body, mind, and spirit cannot effectively go where my passion verse dictates—to the next generation.

So it's time to step away and move into the next chapter.

Learning the step away early was essential to longevity. How can this happen in your ministry?

1. Purchase *Strength Finder 2.0* by Tom Rath[16], read the first thirty-one pages, take the inventory, and read the descriptive passages about your signature themes. Pay careful attention to those striving strengths that, if overplayed, could turn you into a workaholic.

2. Learn to gauge your personal indicators so you'll know when the pressure is building. What symptoms indicate overloaded circuits? Who can tell you face to face that your synapses aren't firing efficiently?

3. Find a place where you can escape the moment and rest.

4. Sanctify a time when you can step away regularly. Many denominations, state conventions, associations, and churches have locales where ministers and their families can vacation at reduced prices or slip away for a few days. Check with your affiliations and ask about them.

5. Call the doctor and schedule a complete physical. Your body may be speaking to you.

Add This to Your Lesson File: WDJD

So a couple of years ago, the WWJD fad rippled across the spiritual landscape and had us all asking, "What would Jesus do?" It wasn't an evil trend and actually resulted in many Americans, even those outside the influence of a local church, asking serious spiritual questions about some of the more mundane issues of life.

For example, a friend had a longstanding smoking habit, several packs a day. His fifteen-year-old daughter gave him a nice silver cigarette lighter for his birthday. It was engraved on both sides and the top with the letters WWJD. Every time he lit a cigarette, he was confronted with the question, "WWJD?" In a matter of months, he quit smoking, cold turkey.

It was a rhetorical question, to speculate what Jesus would do in a given set of circumstances. Just the same, the answers were often relative to that person's life experience or his or her general perspective on the issue at hand. Sometimes the answers were supported by Scripture. But most often, the fad gave us occasion to provide what appeared to be spiritual answers without the truth of Scripture.

It's an unnecessary question anyway: "What would Jesus do?" How often do we tackle life problems by asking the wrong questions? The right question is "what did Jesus do?" We have Scripture as a measure of His life and can find answers to the most perplexing problems right there. Not only that, but also, if He actually lives in us and we have the mind of Christ as purported in the New Testament, there's not so much guesswork in determining the directions we take in life.

With three hundred ministers leaving the ministry every month and with so many churches in survival mode, perhaps those of us in ministry should more closely mimic Him and follow the steps He took to the finish line. It isn't so much forecasting and prediction. We should just follow in His steps.

Chapter 4

Distance
What He's Doing in the Long Haul

Where I am going you cannot follow Me now, but you will follow later.
—John 13:36

et's all embrace Simon Peter, our blood brother and soul mate. He's the biblical character with whom a good many of us readily identify, the apostle we all love. We read about him and see ourselves. It's because the truth about him is also the truth about us. He was impetuous, impulsive, impatient, and till the day of Pentecost, spiritually impotent. His legend, however, inspires and challenges us. Early in our biblical educations, we learn he's the one most aligned with us average Joes.

The backstory of his eventual death is truly inspiring. They say he left Rome during a time of intense persecution under Roman emperor Nero. On the roadway out of town, he met the risen Lord Jesus. He said, "Domine quo vadis?" (Lord, where are you going?) Jesus is said to have replied, "Romam vado iterum crucifigi"(I am going to Rome to be crucified again). At that,

Peter turned, went back to Rome, and was crucified. He is said to have refused to die on a cross like Jesus, unworthy to be the recipient of such an honor. The legend says he died on an upside-down cross instead.[1] He went the distance to fulfill Christ's call.

Interestingly, a church was built to memorialize the place where Peter turned and went back to Rome to die. It is the Chapel of the Domine Quo Vadis, also known as the Church of St. Mary in Palmis, constructed in 1637. A guarded marble slab in the center of the church replicates the footprints of Jesus, marking the place when Peter turned to go back to Rome. Even in legend, the epoch of Peter is the story of important pivot points that signal changes in his service to Christ.[2]

Simon Peter Was a Long-term Project

There's a beach on the northwestern shore of the Sea of Galilee that is, at least for me, among the most memorable Holy Land sites. It was a location known intimately to Simon Peter and would have been familiar to the contemporaries of Christ as well. For Simon Peter, while it may have been an integral part of his daily routine, it marked two important turning points in his life, his first and last encounters with Jesus. As mentioned briefly in chapter 1, it was the place where Jesus called Peter and his brother Andrew. Then, after the resurrection, it was where Jesus restored Peter and, according to Roman Catholic tradition, announced his primacy. The words Jesus spoke to him there, "Follow me," framed his life.

A fourth-century church, the Church of the Primacy of Peter was constructed near that beach. Inside the chapel is a rock called the *mensa Christi*, the table of Christ, where our Lord is said to have fed grilled fish to His apostles during the third post-resurrection appearance. At the shoreline in front of the church, someone in the early ninth century imbedded six heart-shaped stones in the sand to commemorate the apostles and memorialize Christ's questions to Peter: "Do you love me? Do you love me? Do you love me?" (John 21:15, 16, 17). There's also a gorgeous bronze statue depicting Christ's restoration of Peter. In every way, this stop on the tour of Galilee is sensory overload, an emotional and spiritual rush. No place touches me as deeply, with the exception of the empty tomb. It's been chill-bump time for me in each of our seven visits there.

The church and markers remind me of Peter's failure, restoration, and the three-year work Jesus was accomplishing in him. At the center of Peter's call and time with the Lord is a central truth: Peter was being taught the character of Christ. As they traveled and ministered together, Jesus was forming His own character in Simon Peter. It was a project of distance, a work Jesus was doing in him over the long haul. Two millennia later, Jesus is attempting that work in each person called into His service. He asks us to go the distance in ministry too so He can form His character in us. Like Peter, we know there are no shortcuts, bypasses, or work-arounds. It's the full agenda of our relationship with Him. That's the reason alarming numbers of ministers leaving the ministry each month is such an arresting truth. Many leave before they actually begin. Most leave before He's finished with them.

Much of the biblical interplay between Jesus and Peter substantiates the way Jesus was shaping Simon Peter for future use. One incident in particular illustrates the total change Jesus was introducing in Peter's thought patterns, life direction, and leadership. It occurred in a text very familiar to us, when Jesus asked the apostles a most important question. The conversation between Jesus, the disciples, and ultimately Simon Peter is recorded in Matthew 16:13–19. In a brilliant use of language, Jesus showed Simon Peter where he was going. It is a profound word picture that, above most of the others, reveals the deep work Jesus was doing in the man known as *protos*, that is, first. Jesus asked,

> "Who do people say that the Son of Man is?"
> And they said, "Some say John the Baptist; others Elijah; still others, Jeremiah, or one of the prophets."
> "But you," He asked them, "who do you say that I am?"
> Simon Peter answered, "You are the Messiah, the Son of the living God."
> And Jesus responded. "Simon, son of Jonah, you are blessed because flesh and blood did not reveal this to you, but my Father in heaven. And I also say that you are Peter, and on this Rock I will build My church and the forces of Hades will not overpower it."

Let's get inside the text for a moment. Before we do, however, let me offer a disclaimer. Please know my basic lack of scholarship into the finer nuances of biblical languages. They fascinate me, and I truly love learning about them. My master of divinity diploma is annotated "with languages," meaning I took more than basic courses in both Greek and Hebrew. But I'm a novice here, way over my head and beyond my pay grade. Still, knowing the power of the words Jesus used thrills me. Join my feeble excursion through them.

Jesus promised to change Peter's name. But the change would be far deeper than a mere handle. In a brilliant use of words, Jesus promised to alter the course of Peter's life. He was going to reshape Simon bar Jonah into *Petros*, rock.[3] It's interesting and revealing to note the word *Jonah* actually means "dove."[4] Since every word in the New Testament is a word picture, the use of a term like "dove" in this context must be a more comprehensive image, larger than a single restrictive use. Of course, "dove" usually projects the thought of "peace." At a deeper level though, "dove" can represent every bird species. In this broader context, it refers to the flighty, instinctive, highly social, migratory character of avian vertebrates. Birds have nesting instincts but are most attuned to flight. People who watch them must be patient and steady, as birds are apt to fly away at the slightest movement. So the name "bar Jonah," a patriarchal connection to Peter and Andrew's father, may have depicted old John as a man of peace. But used of Simon, it was more descriptive of his impulsive, flighty nature. Search it out! None of the Gospel writers were inspired to refer to his brother Andrew as "Andrew bar Jonah." The "bar Jonah" image is a picture of a fluttering bird. It was distinctly characteristic of Simon.

Jesus promised Peter he would change him to "rock," "Petros." There's certainly been a good bit of study of this word, most of it focused on whether or not Peter is the rock upon which Christ's church is to be constructed. In this particular context, I'd prefer to ease past that trip wire and take the usual Protestant angle: Peter's faith, revealed to him by the Father in heaven, was the foundational underpinning of the church Jesus is building. After two millennia of study and debate, churchmen cannot rectify the divide created by the Lord's statement: "Upon this Rock I will build my church." The Catholics must cling to their interpretation because it is the bedrock of apostolic succession, their claims to papal primacy, their system of hierarchical authority, and title deed to *the* church. Those of the reformed tradition must reject Peter's supremacy for much the same reasons, from an opposite point of view.

The argument misses the point anyway. Like many theological debates, the wrong question has dominated the discussion. The text isn't about who will be the head of the church. Jesus is the head. No, the real topic of that passage is the character work Jesus announced in Peter and, subsequently, in those He calls to serve His kingdom purposes. With pinpoint accuracy, Jesus identified the basic trouble spot in Peter's character and announced His plan to rebuild Peter so that he could go the distance in fulfilling his purpose as a disciple of Christ.

The contrasting images depicted by Christ's graphic words are profound. Jesus would transform Peter from a fluttering, instinctive flyer to a solid, weighty, perhaps immovable rock. He would be changed from the delicate bone structure of an avian to the substantial weight of stone. The shoot-from-the-hip blunderbuss would be changed into a dependable, courageous spokesperson. It was a thrilling announcement then, especially as Jesus revealed the Father's redemptive plan. Today, the prospects of what Jesus intends to change in those He calls to spiritual leadership is equally sensational. Since He knows us in our mother's womb and wires us for life, this is His goal for called servants in the length and breadth of their kingdom purpose. He wants to transform us to be like Him. He aims to construct His character in each of us.

The Gospels and the book of Acts record the various elements or stages of this transformation. Simon Peter was back and forth. His character alternated between momentous highs and gut-wrenching lows. In one moment the rock was visible, in another the fluttering bird. At times Jesus would applaud him and at other times give him a reprimand. It was a process of spiritual growth that moved Him back and forth between the extremes of his old self and the expected outcomes of the new. Note the swaying motion:

> Then Peter replied to Him, "Explain this parable to us." "Are even you still lacking in understanding?" He asked.
> —Matthew 15:15–16

> "You are blessed because flesh and blood did not reveal this to you, but my Father in heaven."
> —Matthew 16:17

> But He turned and told Peter, "Get behind Me, Satan! You are an offense to Me because you're not thinking about God's concerns, but man's."
> —Matthew 16:23

> Then Peter came to Him and said, Lord, how many times could my brother sin against me and I forgive him? As many as seven times?" "I tell you, not as many as seven," Jesus said to him, "but 70 times seven."
> —Matthew 18:21–22

> "Simon, Simon, look out! Satan has asked to sift you like wheat. But I have prayed for you that your faith may not fail. And you, when you have turned back, strengthen your brothers." "Lord," he told Him, "I'm ready to go with you both to prison and to death." "I tell you, Peter," He said, "the rooster will not crow today until you deny three times that you know Me."
> —Luke 22:31–34

> Then He came and found them sleeping. "Simon, are you sleeping?" He asked Peter. "Couldn't you stay awake one hour?"
> —Mark 14:37

Then Simon Peter, who had a sword, struck the high priest's slave and cut off his right ear. The slaves name was Malchus. At that, Jesus said to Peter, "Sheathe your sword! Am I not to drink the cup the Father has given Me?"

—John 18:10–11

And there are others. Notable among them are two verses that haunt me two thousand years after they were written. Though Peter's name isn't mentioned in the first of them, they are both significant in understanding his wavering, unreliable nature. Matthew wrote, "Then all the disciples deserted Him and fled" (Matthew 26:56). Then, as Jesus was led away by the mob, Doctor Luke reminds us, "Meanwhile Peter was following at a distance" (Luke 22:54). These two verses portray a frightened, laid-back, reluctant, perhaps confused man. It was the flip side of the other Peter, the one with the sword, the one who had said he would go die with Jesus. Would the real Peter please stand up!

As *protos*, that is, first, among the apostles, Jesus went to his house, used his boat, and addressed him more often than the others. Peter was our Lord's prime project. He would become the most important human in the early church because Jesus had chosen Peter to be the recipient of His most intimate and urgent character development. But it was a project that could only be finalized in the long haul. Peter had to go the distance. Even as Jesus prepared to die, the character project was incomplete. Take note of this conversation between them:

"Lord, "Simon Peter said to Him, "where are you going?"

Jesus answered, "Where I am going you cannot follow Me now, but you will follow later."

"Lord," Peter asked, "why can't I follow You now? I will lay down my life for You."

Jesus replied. "Will you lay down your life for Me? A
rooster will not crow until you have denied Me three times."
—John 13:36–38

Here was Peter, the fluttering bird, at his impulsive best.
Arrogant and boastful at this earlier point in the narrative, he
indicated a readiness to die for and with Christ. But he really
wasn't ready. The character of Christ wasn't formed in Him.
There were lessons and a final encounter that would change him
into solid stone. But not yet. There were important events from
which he would learn the final traits of Christ's character.

Pause for a minute. Lay aside all the grails, academic robes,
and symbols of holiness. Who among us doesn't dream of
something greater than the situation entrusted to us? Many
highly qualified, educated servants wonder why they're stuck in a
place or situation far below their expectations. I can't tell you how
many ministers I've counseled as they've struggled in relative
anonymity, serving Him with distinction and faithfulness in an
out-of-the-way ministry assignment. Typically, many of them
want to know why God doesn't move them to a more productive,
higher-paying, or more visible place of service. Don't pretend you
haven't wondered yourself!

Surely, we can't fathom the mysteries of His providence.
Serving Him at all is a supernatural reality few of us can really
fathom. But there is a possibility that, like Peter, we're not ready
for the next chapter. There's still character development to be
done, and we must stay in place while He does it. That's one of
the troubling things about the number of pastors leaving the
ministry every month. By stepping away, they have missed the
remaining preparation He had planned for them. There's more
to be done. We must remain in place so He can do it.

Genuine Pivot Points

Three pivot points asterisk the final elements of Peter's transformation. Had his journey been short-circuited in any way, he may not have become the solid, dependable leader so central in the book of Acts. The first of them took place in the courtyard of Caiaphas, the high priest. Jesus had been arrested and was moving through the Roman checkpoints of trial. Interestingly, only Luke recorded the electric connection that ramped up Peter's learning. In the third accusation of being with Jesus,

> But Peter said, "Man I don't know what you're talking about!" Immediately, while he was still speaking, a rooster crowed. Then the Lord turned and looked at Peter. So Peter remembered the word of the Lord, how He had said to Him, "Before the rooster crows today, you will deny me three times."
>
> And he went outside and wept bitterly.
>
> —Luke 22: 60–62

There was an instant, the briefest second, when their eyes met. I've always wondered what passed between them as their eyes, the windows to their souls, collided. What a poignant moment. Then again, a part of me resists trying to recapture that look. Why speculate about what transpired in them as they connected? It's not such a mystery. We've all had moments of clarity when a lesson was finally learned, a truth was revealed, or when we shared a knowing look with another person. That Peter wept bitterly after their eye contact is enough to let me know the intensity of that look. Luke doesn't give us their impressions or even a clue to the unspoken truth that they shared. But it was intense, a turning point for Peter.

Maybe it was a reckoning for Peter, that one brief nanosecond when the truth about his volatile, unpredictable character finally registered. Jesus had been right about him. He really was a fluttering bird. The swashbuckler slipped into the background, skulking in the shadows, sleeping through an hour when the Master dropped sweat like blood. The look that connected them was most likely a split second of self-awareness. He wept bitterly because he met himself in that look.

Peter's character development took a definitive turn right there. The penetrating eyes of Jesus and the bitter tears he shed seemed to raise a new resolve in him, a new direction with a more definitive outcome. Three days later, when the women announced the empty tomb, this new Peter raced to the tomb, so eager was he to reconnect with the Lord he had so recently denied. When Jesus wasn't there, Peter left Jerusalem and traveled to the Galilee, to the familiar beach of his first meeting with Jesus, to reestablish his spiritual bearings, where he and brother Andrew had fished so often. It was a new chapter in Peter's epoch, the final chapters of his personal growth.

Going the distance in ministry may, in fact, require many self-awareness shocks like Peter's. Several grabbed my attention over the years and impressed lasting lessons about me. Dealing with them not only opened my eyes, but also propelled me another step forward in the character-building project He was attempting to accomplish in me. An early one was particularly painful. A young woman in our church asked me to pray for her mother, suffering from pancreatic cancer. Later, she asked me to visit her mother, which I quickly promised to do. Somehow my note to visit her got lost in the shuffle, and I never got around to it. She soon died. It was an excruciating lesson about me that almost ended that pastorate. Even more, I nearly left the ministry. He taught me the seriousness of keeping promises I had made and the danger of church door conversations. Like Peter, my spirit was willing, but my flesh was weak. I learned something important for the distance.

The second pivot point happened on that very beach at what is known today as Tabgha, Israel. I mentioned it in the "Simon was a long-term project" section of this chapter. What happened there was the culmination of what had to have been an intense few days for Simon Peter and Christ's other followers. There's a very comprehensive accounting of those days in the four Gospels. For the sake of brevity and to accomplish my own ends, I have combined elements of each, and established a basic timeline of what happened in the days leading up to their reunion.

> **Point One:** Jesus was raised from the dead.
>
> **Point Two:** At the news, Peter and John ran to the tomb.
>
> **Point Three:** The tomb was empty, and they didn't see Jesus.
>
> **Point Four:** Disappointed, Peter left Judea and traveled to Galilee.
>
> **Point Five:** He went to the familiar beach where he and his brother had fished and where Jesus had first spoken to them.
>
> **Point Six:** Jesus appeared to the apostles in the upper room. I personally don't think Peter was among them at the first appearance since he's not specifically mentioned by name in the text. Being *protos* (first) among the apostles, that is, the first in every biblical list, Peter's presence would have been annotated had he been present.
>
> **Point Seven:** Jesus appeared to the disciples the second time and confirmed the resurrection with doubting

Thomas. Once again, Peter is not identified as being present with them.

His third post-resurrection appearance happened on the shores of the Sea of Tiberias, where the Church of the Primacy of Peter is now located. Peter had gone there to perhaps reflect and come to grips with the serious turn in his service of Christ. He invited the others to go fishing. While they were fishing, John recognized Jesus on the shore. John said, "It is the Lord." In his excitement, Peter gathered his robing, dove into water, and swam to shore. John 21:15–23 is a verbatim of their conversation, what is generally referred to as the restoration of Peter.

It is interesting to note John's careful selection of words in reference to Peter. In the verses up to John 21:19, he is called Simon Peter. After the restoration, at verse 20, he is only called Peter. Even the disciple Jesus loved noted something different about Peter after his private times with Jesus.

Peter was forgiven, reminded of what Jesus had said to him on their first encounter, and given the charge to feed, shepherd, and care for His sheep. John vividly expressed the final aspect of Simon Peter's character development in his use of Simon's new name, twice.

> Peter turned around and saw the disciple Jesus loved following them.
> —John 21:20

> When Peter saw him, he said to Jesus, "Lord—what about him?"
> —John 21:21

Here's the deal about this focal point. Peter's denial of Christ was a momentous failure. It could have ended Peter's spiritual leadership and service to the kingdom. But we know Peter was a long-term character-development project. His bitter tears could have meant suicide or perhaps murder at the hands of one of the other disciples, banishment from among the inner circle, or at the least a self-imposed spiritual hibernation. Instead, Jesus found him, restored him, and solidified his character to become the most influential person in the apostolic period.

There's another interesting twist, and I can't ignore it. It's a footnote to the thrilling narrative of Christ's resurrection and appearances to His disciples. Obviously, Peter was eager to locate Jesus. That he wanted to make things right after the denial is without doubt a huge, compelling factor. But as is just as clear in the several texts, he did not find Jesus. For whatever reason, he left Judea and traveled up the Jordan Valley to the northwest shore of the Sea of Galilee. Eventually the other disciples joined him there. Then Jesus found Peter.

Oops. Here's another land mine in the work Jesus wants to do in us. Here's this superhero-pastor complex that drives us to fix things ourselves, to be the engineers of our own character development. Let's improve our resume, add another degree, work our way into favor or back into favor, and try to solve our character flaws. Jesus found Peter and touched him at a new place. When he left Tabgha, he was different. The Peter after that time on the beach was stronger, more certain, fearless, and truly ready to die. He tried to find the answer. Jesus, instead, found him.

Like Peter, failure and trouble stalk the people He calls to serve Him. Since we have this treasure in jars of clay, we're not shielded from human error, poor judgment, sinful attitudes, or stupid mistakes. As the rain falls on the just and unjust alike, good things happen to bad people, and bad things happen to good. In the process of character development, we're going to mess up. At times, our messes can be consequential. They can end our journey or enhance it. Sadly, our kingdom service ends most abruptly when we try to be the source of our recovery. But the one who calls us is faithful. He chose us and will be the one who finds us in our distress.

Some mistakes can send us packing. There are consequences to our actions. Most departures from ministry, however, aren't the result of unforgivable error—moral failure, financial malfeasance, theft, legal charges, or some other grievous sin. Usually we walk away because we can't forgive ourselves or accept forgiveness and restoration from others or from Him. The sin of unforgiveness works both ways. Forgiving and being forgiven are consequential steps in our character development.

In each of our visits to Tabgha, I've isolated myself from our travel group to sit alone on the beach. My mind traces the events that happened there and tries to appropriate the forgiveness and restoration of Jesus into my own life and ministry. As I run through a long catalog of my own errors and sins, I ask for Him to complete His character development in me. Every time, I leave that place changed.

He doesn't want me to simply walk away when things have taken a wrong turn. He chose me, and I'm His long-term project. There are those pivot moments when I can recognize my character flaws, come to terms with them, face the humiliation or embarrassment of making a mess of things, and then permit Him the task of correction and continued character development. His work is done in the distance. It's one of the reasons we need to accentuate the finish line of ministry, allowing Him to shape us over the long haul of our kingdom service.

The third pivot point is actually comprised of several related events in the book of Acts. They indicate the finished product of

Peter's character development. The solid, dependable, rock-like persona prepared Peter to eventually die on an upside-down cross. It is notable because it was a long-term project that prepared him to go the distance in kingdom service.

It's interesting that he is called only Peter in most of Acts. The three exceptions are in three references in Acts 10. There, the text identifies him as "Simon, who is also named Peter" (Acts 10:5, 18, 32). Since he was residing with Simon the tanner at Caesarea, it seems the references are for clarification between the two men rather than a recollection of his wavering character. Every other reference to Peter identifies him as such. They signal the completion of his character development. Two verses accentuate Peter's new character.

> But Peter stood up with the eleven, raised his voice, and proclaimed to them ...
>
> —Acts 2:14

> But Peter and the apostles replied, "We must obey God rather than men."
>
> —Acts 5:29

That Luke used a Greek term translated "but" in both instances is worth another pause. Evidently, the two situations were moving in another direction, and Peter did something against the flow. It's notable that he was now, in both circumstances, seen in a leadership position. The man who had slept in the garden, fled the scene of Christ's arrest, followed the mob procession from a distance, and denied Jesus three times was now (1) standing in front of a multitude of mockers, and (2) speaking boldly to the highest court in the land. The fluttering bird wasn't fluttering so much now.

Both are worthy of further comment. The first instance was on the day of Pentecost. Thousands of people were gathered for the Jewish celebration. It was a chaotic experience when "suddenly a sound like that of a rushing wind came from heaven, and it filled the whole house where they were staying. And tongues, like flames of fire that were divided, appeared to them and rested on each one of them" (Acts 2:2–3). In the confusion of such astounding circumstances, the people were perplexed, accusing the believers of being drunk with wine. Luke wrote, "But Peter stood up with the eleven" (Acts 2:14).

Peter didn't slip into the crowd or flutter to the edges. He stood and preached what is thought to be one of the greatest sermons in history. Three thousand people confessed faith in Christ at the end of his message. The image of a flighty, fearful Simon was replaced by one of a confident, strong Peter. The character development of Peter was notched up another level.

Acts 5 records the time when Peter and John were scolded, warned, and eventually flogged for continuing to preach in the name of Jesus. They had previously been arrested and jailed for disobeying the Sadducees' order to stop proclaiming the resurrection (Acts 4:1–4). After an angel miraculously released them from prison (Acts 5:17–21), they were transferred to the Sanhedrin for punishment. They were once again ordered not to preach or teach in the name of Jesus. That's when Peter and the apostles replied, "We must obey God rather than men" (Acts 5:29). They were flogged, giving thanks for suffering, and released. It was another of those character-revealing tests. The fluttering bird Peter might have flitted away, frightened by the harsh motion of the crowd, the strong words of the court. The intimidation meter was registering extreme highs about that time. But, instead, the rock stood and spoke. He so encouraged the others that they all echoed his words.

In all, Peter learned the truth about himself, the forgiveness and restoration of Jesus after an enormous failure, the character development Jesus promised and fulfilled in his life. They occurred over time, incorporated Peter's successes and failures, and prepared Peter to be the voice of the early New Testament church, accomplished in the length and breadth of his personal life.

Loving Peter isn't hard for me. His feet of clay challenge and encourage me. More than anything, I'm inspired by his vision, endurance, and belief in what Jesus would accomplish in him. These qualities, and a long list of others, kept him from walking away when an exit would have seemed a more appropriate move. Evidently, he understood the mystery of His call at a level that overshadowed his wavering, fluttering ways. Every two years, I get to sit on that beach at Tabgha, think through the character development He's doing in my life, and remember that the fulfillment of His call is more about Him than it is about me.

What about the work He is doing in your life?

1. What are your character flaws? If you don't know, perhaps you should ask Him to show them to you. Can you handle a come-to-Jesus meeting?

2. Admit it. You've made mistakes too. What is the most grievous error in your ministry? Have you sought restoration? Can you handle a restoration process?

3. Are you weary of the journey? Did you think it would take this long to find traction in ministry? Are you equipped for the long haul?

4. Can you think of two common images that may illustrate the character development Jesus is doing in your life? Think about the fluttering bird and the solid rock. Does something as vivid come to mind in defining you?

5. Have you ever thought about seeking another career? Read Romans 11:29. What does that say to you?

Kick
Endurance for the Finish

When the days were coming to a close for Him to be taken up, He determined to journey to Jerusalem.

—LUKE 9:51

everal years ago our staff attended a church health conference, a schedule of power-packed worship, a well-known keynote speaker, and high-octane breakout sessions especially convened for turnaround churches. One of the breakout sessions was facilitated by the pastor of a large, mega turnaround church. In the Q&A following his high-tech, contemporary presentation, someone asked, "What happened to instigate the turnaround?" His answer startled everybody in the room. He said, "We decided to turn it around." After an uncomfortable silence, he laid it out for us.

1. God is as powerful in their community as He is in any community in the world. He said that the God who is

working miracles in India and China is the same God who guides the church in Any Town, USA. Who can argue with that?

2. God designed His church to effectively minister in the community in which it was planted. His point seemed to be what I implied in an earlier chapter: there's nothing wrong with the church.

3. God has given His people what they need to fulfill the mission of the church in every community.

4. Mission is a "want-to" issue for every local congregation. If the churches are in decline or plateaued, which seems to be systemic today, it is because the people have decided themselves to take ownership of the church and go their own routes.

His conclusion: God had provided everything needed for their church to thrive in its ministry setting. The only remaining element to reconnect the church to the community around them was their decision to intentionally pursue their stated mission. So they decided they would.

As you might imagine, this was the topic of discussion during the drive back to our church. Everybody weighed in. For the most part, we all thought the guy was presumptuous and arrogant. His confidence seemed to step over a line, translating to the other ministers in the room as swagger. Yes, we all oohed and aahed the impressive statistics about his church's resurgence. But "we decided to turn it around" came across to most of us as some off-brand humanistic hype, the stuff of the executive boardroom, again.

In subsequent weeks, "we decided to turn it around" stayed fixed in my mind. The pastor had a point. And the longer I reflected on it, the more it made sense. Perhaps it was the crisis of faith Henry Blackaby wrote about in *Experiencing God*[1], years ago. That study was a life changer for many individuals and congregations as well. In Unit 7, Blackaby wrote, "When God tells me what He wants to do through me, I will face a crisis of belief."[2] In Unit 8, the thought is advanced. He wrote, "You cannot stay where you are and go with God"[2]. The entire idea is that to fully experience God, we have to join Him in what He is doing in our lives. To achieve that end, we must decide to make the move. He makes the invitation, gives us what we need to obey, and expects us to take the necessary moves to do so, no matter the cost. So after some thought, further discussion, and Bible study, "we decided to turn it around" seemed less a boast about human accomplishment and more a strategic reality of mission.

That was before intent was church buzz or the term *missional* was in vogue. Since then, as the shift from church growth to church health to church mission is being finalized, the idea of purpose is commonly viewed as essential to the fulfillment of His assignment. Vision, core values, and mission clarity are now part and parcel of church strategy. Suddenly, missional is the word, the thrilling realization that every church member is a missionary strategically deployed to fulfill the mission of the local congregation and the kingdom mission that unites all churches. Looking back, the breakout group leader that made our jaws drop from such an apparent self-absorbed declaration was actually on the leading edge of a movement. Mission had moved up a notch. We were becoming "purpose driven."[3]

Intent in the Mission of Jesus

It's not such a revolutionary concept, intent. The language of the New Testament advances the ministry of Jesus and the early church in power words like *compelled, directed, guided, preach, teach,* and *power*; connectors like *must, all things, never,* and *always*; and specific directional markers like Jerusalem, Judea, Samaria, and *the uttermost parts of the world.* Doors were opened and closed, schedules were altered, miracles happened, power was given, people were called up for service, and many other clear examples occurred of meaningful adherence to a plan—His plan.

Luke's orderly account provides a point-by-point notation of Christ's intent. Reading through his twenty-four chapters is almost like reading a travelogue, annotated, outlined, and compiled with the accuracy and detail of a medical record. Nine verses from Chapters 9–19 indicate the aim of His trip. There were opportunities to teach, heal, and minister as they moved from Galilee, through Samaria, and up to Jerusalem. Each of the summary verses that mark their way to Jerusalem is neatly numbered in every one of my worn Bibles. When obstacles blocked the path or when there was a distraction, these verses encouraged me to press on. They remind me of the need for purposeful intent in my own personal ministry. Following Him means doing what He does the way he did it and with the heart and mind that compelled Him.

> When the days were coming to a close for Him to be taken up, He determined to journey to Jerusalem.
>
> —Luke 9:51

> While they were traveling, He entered a village and a woman named Martha welcomed Him into her home.
>
> —Luke 10:38

> He went through one town and village after another, teaching and making His way to Jerusalem.
>
> —Luke 13:22

Yet, I must travel today, tomorrow, and the next day, because it is not possible for a prophet to perish outside of Jerusalem.

—Luke 13:33

Now, great crowds were traveling with Him.

—Luke 14:25

While traveling to Jerusalem He passed between Samaria and Galilee.

—Luke 17:11

He entered Jericho and was passing through.

—Luke 19:1

When He had said these things, He went on ahead, going up to Jerusalem.

—Luke 19:28

As He approached and saw the city, He wept over it.

—Luke 19:41

My first notice of these verses was in a King James Version, and for reference and emphasis, I still love the reading of it. The KJV reads, "And it came to pass, when the time was come that he should be received up, he steadfastly set his face to go to Jerusalem" (Luke 9:51). That "He steadfastly set His face" seems to so fit the context of such single-minded pursuit. That Jesus was so focused on the work the Father had given Him is such a thrilling statement about mission. Each of the verses pictures a stop along the way, a momentary interruption of His journey. The language Luke used made it abundantly clear that Jesus and the entourage were on the move, traveling, passing through, aimed at the Holy City. Luke made me understand that Jesus was focused on the completion of His work in Jerusalem. Everything else was incidental.

Translation Please

Intent is another important element of longevity in ministry. To know that Jesus persisted in a single-minded journey to the city of His death encourages me to aim at something beyond what is happening right now. A sense of determination may be the final kick needed to envision the finish line and strive toward it. Translating what Jesus did two thousand years ago to the current occasion of ministers leaving their calling every month is to apply several connecting realities:

> **Reality One:** Jesus is to be my example for ministry service.
>
> **Reality Two:** Our Lord was very intent in finishing the work the Father had assigned.
>
> **Reality Three:** The Son of Man modeled human character traits for the fulfillment of His Father's assignment.
>
> **Reality Four:** Jesus Christ promised His presence to those who follow Him.
>
> **Reality Five:** He promised us supernatural power in following Him.

There's some culture confusion too, admiration of traits that keep us in the game but with a wrong motive. Recently I was invited into a church squabble. The pastor, mission organization leadership, and finance committee were gridlocked in three opinions about funding a summer mission project. They wanted me to referee. What fun. When I met with the pastor, finance committee chair, and mission committee leader, they were all immovable. Each said he or she was being steadfast in holding his or her ground. After hearing all their arguments, I told them they weren't being steadfast, but stubborn. And there's a difference. Steadfastness is a spiritual virtue, representing Him in the process. Stubbornness, on the other hand, is self-gratifying. In short order, they resolved their issues and constructed a nice, new, modern playground, a bridge to their ever-growing community.

Surely, Jesus isn't cultivating stubbornness in us, the ones He called to service. No, intent, purpose, determination, persistence, endurance, and mission comprise the right stuff of distance in ministry, not stubbornness. When the grind wears us down and the finish line is obscured by the hard stuff, the spiritual virtues Jesus is attempting to form in us give us the kick necessary to go on. It's the same effect that compels distance runners toward the finish line, the surge of energy that pushes them forward when they hit the proverbial wall.

Over the years, I've worked with more than a few ministers whose pastoral service was sacrificed on the altar of self-centered obstinacy. One pastor boasted about being a "bulldog." He quoted what Sir Winston Churchill was supposed to have said about bulldogs. He said the bulldog's angled face was designed so he could breathe and hold on at the same time.[4] So when he claimed a bulldog spirit, he was defining an immovable, hard-scrapple attitude. He communicated negative vibes to me, making me wonder how he came across to his church family.

Perhaps a biblical metaphor would transmit a better idea of steadfastness. Of course, we're in church so the picture is Jesus and not a squirrel. But even He showed us a more appropriate image of intent and purpose. That would be the *doulos*,[5] the Greek concept of slave. Whether captured in conquest, enslaved by indebtedness, or actually purchased for the purpose of serving, the *doulos* was totally focused on his master. Christ's followers are bought with a price and are therefore totally motivated by obedience to the master. Steadfastness, then, is a total absorption to the will and instruction of the master. It is seeing the master's instructions to the very end, absolute obedience until the work is completed.

There was one memorable incident where these traits just about ended the pastoral service of a friend. Honestly, I can't remember the issue. So it must not have been of great spiritual significance. But the pastor had told the congregation, perhaps a little rashly, that he would resign if they persisted in a decision they had made. When they went right ahead, he felt he would have to follow through with his resignation. It really created a dilemma for them all. He really didn't want to quit, his poor wife was about to have a nervous breakdown, and the church didn't really expect him to follow through. But he said, "I told them I would resign, and I must keep my word."

Well, I told him he was being stubborn. So I advised him to let it pass so he could be steadfast in fulfilling his vow to them, to God, and to his family when he accepted their call to lead them. So he told them he had spoken in the heat of the moment, asked their forgiveness for being so fast on the draw, and moved on through many years of effective leadership and service.

Going the distance means allowing Jesus to do the character development that permits us to serve His intended purpose. When we walk away in a huff, usually because we're too stubborn, what He is doing in us is short-circuited. How many great ministry careers are abbreviated because we use the wrong paradigm as a model for our service?

His Way or the Highway

All of these character traits are bullet points of spiritual maturity. So often, the distance seems out of reach because we have a dysfunctional concept of spiritually mature leadership. In many instances, the boardroom is more visible than the prayer room, and the traits we seek are more borrowed from Wall Street than the Via Dolorosa. One of the most harmful approaches of secular leadership models is the my-way-or-the-highway attitude so prevalent in the captains of industry.

Of course, the five steps of going the distance mentioned in chapter 3 are designed to fix our agendas on His way rather than our ways. We've all read the material about knowing what mountain to die on and deciding how to sift through competing ideas. If there is one lesson we could learn from the Lord, it would be His total and absolute surrender to His Father's will. It marked every moment of Jesus's life and ministry, a submission to the Father that moderated His every step, word, thought, and action.

Such a viewpoint gave Jesus the long view of ministry service. As previously mentioned, He could see the joys that were before Him. What is more, those joys enabled Him to endure until He had completed God's redemptive plan and announce, "It is finished." He knew with certainty the mountain He would die on and therefore aimed everything toward finishing what the Father gave Him to do. In it all, there was steadfastness, intent, purpose, and mission. For Jesus, it was always His way. It was the highway.

Let's talk about your kick.

1. Would you define yourself as stubborn or steadfast? Remember the New Testament image that best exemplifies steadfastness.
2. How intent are you about life? About your family? Devotional life? About ministry?
3. Have you ever written a mission statement for life? Check out Richard Bolles's book, *How to Write Your Mission Statement for Life.*[6] Do you think a personal mission statement may stimulate purpose and mission in you?
4. On a scale of one to ten, with one being the lowest and ten the highest, how would you rate your personal endurance?

Chapter 6

Finish. Period.

The Joys of Going the Distance

It is finished.

—JOHN 19:30

The ministry dropout rate is alarming and should be unacceptable to us. On the fringes are people who leave kingdom service for legitimate reasons, a long list of aberrant behaviors and missteps that can bring ministry to a sudden halt. Even more, the thicker catalog of departures is more about serving in this crazy postmodern world, the frustrations of churches entrenched in outmoded mechanics, unfulfilled expectations, inadequate financial provision, marriage and family pressures, and so many other systemic ills. But underneath the system, there's a personal element too, intimate facts and truth about the lives destroyed in the most noble pursuit of all, that of serving Him. Our evaluative tools usually identify the overarching structural elements that are really beyond the reach of denominations, conventions, associations, and even books. In a nonhierarchical organization like the Southern Baptist Convention, the work at that level is mostly suggestive and has little authority. Even at that, most of the research and application by our brightest minds addresses organizational solutions. Our start-up engines are aimed at moving the big machinery, with little more than a nudge to the individual pieces.

There are few resources dedicated to the personal elements, the men, women, and children who bear the marks of Christ while serving Him. The lack of resources may be the unmentionable of ministry, factual truth that must remain under the surface. A few convention locations provide short-stay places for refreshment, limited counseling services, some individuals with the heart to help, and occasional churches willing to lend a hand. They are mostly emergency or post-op recovery settings that provide brief periods of healing. But there's little in the way of preventive care, of guidance in clarifying and verifying His call, of preparing individuals for the potholes in the journey, or even rehearsing the joys of going the distance. In the heat of the moment, many people walk away without thinking about the work He is doing in them or the joyful promises He's made to those who finish.

I don't know what He's doing in you, but the character work He's continually doing in me requires an anvil at times. It often involves a beating, something distasteful, or lessons that can only be learned in the crucible. When somebody's turning the thumbscrews on me, I can't always see what's on the next page, between the lines, or under the surface. The urgency of what's right in front of me sends other things to the background. Still, in thirty-four years of pastoral service, practicing the five steps Jesus modeled, realizing the fabulous certainties of His call, and recognizing the character work He's doing in me have taken me to the ocean of His grace so that I could hang around for what's coming next. They were not church projects or large-scale learning outcomes that would alter the community around us. This learning was custom designed for me.

Step aside one more time. Rick Warren's *The Purpose-Driven Life*[1] was a blockbuster for many reasons. Up front was the way Warren's work shattered the egotism of the times. The first sentence in the book boldly stated, "It's not about you."[2] By now, we're all familiar with the many refrains of that anthem, a movement away from self toward Him and then, finally, to others. By now, we're finally realizing, at least in an academic sense, we're not the centers of the universe.

Then, on the other hand, there's Reggie McNeal's book *Get a Life*.[3] The subtitle, *It Is All about You*, moves us to another level of self-awareness. This perspective requires more fine-tuning, an updated version of self-awareness that individualizes and personalizes God's redemptive work in the world by changing us individually. From this angle, it is all about me. It is the enormous cultural truth that change happens on an individual level. Each of us bears the personal burden of having His mind, living His life, and responding to His personal claim over us. Everything in His redemptive plan is geared to the elect, the ones He has chosen, most notably, the ones He has called. The truth lands on me with great force every time I take the bread and the cup. We celebrate the ordinance in a corporate setting, what He ordained for the church. But that bread and that cup are symbols of my importance to His finished work. It blows me away every time. It is about me.

In this regard, the connected dots of lower church influence over culture, exclusion of the church from the marketplace of ideas, the secularization of the world around us, and the growing exodus from kingdom service are micro issues, not macro.

Somewhere in the mix of cultural solutions, we must devise personal strategies, remedies that begin in each one of us and move upward to the structural whole. Solving the mysteries of spiritual impotence in a world like this one radiates from the intent, clear aim, and purpose of the spiritual leader as it infuses the greater body with a sense of mission. To "Finish. Period." is then, an individual process.

Once again, Jesus modeled the personal dynamics designed to propel us to the finish. Scripture affirms that Jesus endured the cross for the joy set before Him. We usually emphasize "endured" because we know the suffering and pain inflicted on Him as he made His way to the cross. When I throw this verse in front of disillusioned, case-hardened friends, they want me to know they're not Jesus, they cannot imagine those joys because, unlike Him, they haven't seen heaven, and God did not intend for them to endure such horrors when He called them.

Perhaps it's the mental conditioning of a softer world, the idea that nothing is supposed to be hard, especially ministry. Instead, we tend to portray the world of kingdom service as streets of gold, pearly gates, crystal seas, pillars, clouds, and the dragon thrown into the burning abyss. The streak of idealism, what Harriet calls my rose-colored glasses, that runs through a good many of us refuses to see the dark side. We generally don't like the hard parts. So don't talk to me about endurance. It's just a code word for difficult tests, and ministry isn't supposed to be a difficult test.

Still, we can agree that serving Him in church or church-related service right now is hard. Once again, it's not hard because the world is worse, the idea of church no longer works, or the truth of Scripture is no longer operative. No, ministry and the people serving in it have been conditioned by the thirty-second sound bite, spur of the moment expectations, instant gratification, and all the other cultural descriptives we use to define our times. It's hard because we perform this kingdom service in a cold, dark world among people who are just as cold and dark. It's hard because ministry pits us against the grain, moves in countercultural motion, and must exist when all the bells and whistles of a highly technical world are in the stands cheering for the other side. Ministry is hard because Jesus said it would be so, on numerous occasions. He promised us the garden of Gethsemane, not a rose garden.

For a moment though, forget the times, census figures, growing number of "nones," and all the dysfunction that clogs the mission machinery of most local churches. Is it possible that individual, personal dynamics are the main cause of ministry dropout? In the process of coaching and mentoring young ministers, training them for service, preparing them for the church and the mission field, could we have overlooked the personal dimensions? While we moan and whine about the unique difficulties of the task, how often do we celebrate the joys of this service? When was the last time you talked to someone about finishing what He called you to do, for the joy set before you?

It's true. Most of the conversation about ministry service involves some mention of endurance, the will to press on, and all the synonyms I used in chapter 5 to describe it: intent, vigilance, purpose, mission, steadfastness, and the rest. So, for a change, reverse the Hebrews verse, and take another slant. "For the joy set before Him He endured." For a moment, put the joy out front. I'm just curious. How would the landscape change if we talked more about the joy and less about the endurance? What would happen if we all pulled a bait and switch with hurting ministers and talked to them about the blessings He promised and His generous provision for our needs as we serve Him? Could the dropout rate be altered by such minor wordplay?

Well Done, Good and Faithful Slave

While I was exploring His call, I sought the counsel of several pastors. They were older, more educated, and seasoned by years of pastoral leadership. Seasoned might be the wrong term here, maybe a little soft. They were actually hardened by their years of service, jaded, if you will. They led larger, multistaff congregations, and they were involved in Baptist life at numerous levels. They were faithful servants in every way. That's why I sought them out. What they said was surprising. Each of them said, as if they had rehearsed it together beforehand, if I could find anything else in this whole wide world to do in life, I should do it, posthaste. The bucket brigade had started, and I was just in the exploratory stages of ministry calling. Their words weren't really discouraging because they didn't actually tell me to run from this thing as fast as I could. But the stars in my eyes were dimmed a little by such a uniform cynicism.

And experience later underscored this less-than-positive veneer. In my second pastorate, I attended a state convention meeting with the pastors of three of the largest, most influential churches in our association. On the drive to Columbia, we stopped at a rest area for refreshment. One of them inquired about my thoughts after riding with three wiser, older men for a couple of hours. I told them, mostly in jest, that I wanted to commit suicide. It had been the most depressing hour in my short ministry experience. To the man, these three griped, complained, groused, and bad-mouthed everything in their churches for two hours up there and two hours back. They talked about their members, deacons, poor giving habits, bylaws, and just about anything you can imagine in church life, even the reverenced cooking so characteristic of Baptist churches. In some instances, they shared a knowing laugh, the been-there, done-that snicker of having had this conversation before. Mostly, anger and bitterness seeped through their humor. Young, idealistic, fresh-out-of-seminary me prayed that I could love and appreciate my church family a little more than that. Even more, I prayed that I wouldn't grow into a bitter old man. Riding in the car with them, my heart fast-forwarded to the finish line. I wanted to finish better.

Years later, finishing period took on a deeper and more profound meaning during a personal crisis. When Dr. David Brandli told me I had stage-four transitional cell carcinoma of the bladder, the finish line flashed across my screen again, this time in a life-altering way. Finishing stronger or better wouldn't be the final stages of ministry for me if this cancer ran its predicted course. Suddenly, at age fifty-four, finishing period was the deal. That day everything that I had previously heard about the "C" word became real. There was an enormous shift in my personal goals and ambitions and in what I determined to be His purposes for my calling. The priorities of life were filtered much differently. Finishing well or finishing strong became secondary to finishing period. With two surgeries and months of chemotherapy on the calendar, my ambitions turned into a compulsion to finish the race at all.

Chapter 1 is about finishing before you start or finishing before you've accomplished what God called you do. Of course, that is central to my personal concern over the number of ministers leaving the ministry every month. The possibility of death introduced a little higher stakes in the finishing conversation.

But still, at least in my personal faith, there are worse things than death. I mean, forgive me, but we do have the promise of eternal life and forever with Jesus to lift us in the uncertainties of cancer, physical deterioration, and eventually death. But to live a life without purpose or meaning or short of what we were intended to do and be seems a little more depressing to me. In fact, after some thought, prayer, and counseling, I adjusted to the death thing, went through the grueling treatments, and am still functioning twelve years later. Thank Him!

But at one time, during a scalding few months of ministry, the thoughts of leaving His service and the calling He issued over my life were more paralyzing to me than the cancer diagnosis. In the cancer thing, we all prayed for healing and His peace through the process. This prayer was shared by the extended family too, friends, our congregation, and a new group of people on my friend list, fellow cancer victims. Underneath, however, I was actually comforted by His many promises and the prospect of Him saying to me, on that day, whether sooner or later, "Well done, good and faithful slave" (Matthew 25:21).

That image of standing at the finish line and hearing His pronouncement over me had another angle too. This angle wasn't as comforting. Call it a guilt trip, negative reinforcement, or a pessimistic take on what's supposed to be more upright or heavenly. It's the picture of standing before Him after I had deserted His call. In this version, there's no reward or congratulatory comments. It's the scolding of a slothful slave who didn't do what the Master commanded. The thought of standing there after a life shortened by cancer was blessed. The same picture, of standing there after abandoning His call, was heartrending. In some of the hard days, Harriet and I agonized over this possibility. The idea that He would ever say to me,

"Well done, good and faithful slave," helped us through some demanding times.

We don't talk about the promises of finishing period often enough. When our colleagues are facing the fiery trials of ministry, we're more apt to nod agreement, tell them we understand, wrap our arms around them, embrace them, and commiserate with their pain. Wanting to ease their burdens or perhaps lighten their load, we're prone to dig up some greeting-card sentiment that just doesn't cut it.

> God isn't going to put on you more than you can handle.
>
> These things have come to pass and not to stay.
>
> When the going gets tough, the tough get going.
>
> God's going to give you a new normal.
>
> You'll be a stronger person when this is all over.

And pages of really kind thoughts that may give us a momentary lift, but rarely clarify the situation.

It almost seems implausible at first. But imagine a scenario when a friend is in the storm, seriously debating whether to leave the ministry, and you start talking about the finish line. Here we're fast-forwarding past the immediacy of the current trial and asking them to aim at a future promise. Maybe, just maybe, we should talk a little more about the joys.

A dear friend gave me what I think is an authentic crown of thorns. It's been displayed in a visible place for many years and today hangs in a conspicuous place in my new home study. Whenever I look up from whatever I'm doing, it grabs my attention. It reminds me throughout every day of His glorious finish. To the world of His day, it was a symbol of death and loss, a criminal's shame. But for those of us who believe, it is the "victor's crown," and that modern song starts playing in my head at the mere sight of it. "He wears the victor's crown, He overcomes, He overcomes."[4] It is an encouraging celebration of the finish, a remembrance of the most stupendous finish in all of human history.

Several weeks ago, Harriet and I took a young minister and his wife to lunch. He had recently been terminated after nearly ten years on the staff of a nearby church. He wasn't given any substantive reasons for his firing, just the common, repeated refrain, "We just want to go in another direction." In this case, it was because someone didn't like him. One of the heavy-hitting, big-giving church members threatened the pastor: it's either him or me. So the young staffer was terminated.

As a result, he and his wife had decided to leave the ministry for good. During our lunch, I asked him a question that we often ignore: Where did he envision being in five or ten years? When I asked him to recount his greatest days in ministry, those times that had affirmed his call and blessed his life, you know what? A spark was ignited in them during that conversation. They dreamed a little, laughed a lot, and shed a few tears while we reminisced and replayed some of the high points of their service. In the aftermath of that two-hour lunch, we enlisted him to serve on our ministry team while they worked through some of the details of life. Suddenly, there was the possibility of a new chapter. It was so refreshing and encouraging to note the ways they remembered His call and refocused on the future. As they say, that's what I'm talking about.

The Test of Whether or Not He's Finished with You

People want to know why I decided to retire. It's one of those hot topics these days. One of my long-term pastor friends told me he was retiring for health reasons: he was sick of the church. It was a joke, I think. Just a few months ago, I read Thom Rainer's blog titled *What Happens When Boomer Pastor's Retire?*[5] Evidently, it's a big deal as the vast baby boomer generation moves through this important generational milestone. His data indicates that a good number of boomer ministers are staying active in their churches past traditional retirement years. We love the refrain "He's not finished with me yet!" Many of us have the T-shirt.

One of the questions people ask is whether I feel as if God is through with me. And, of course, the answer is a loud no. And it's more than just a feeling, sense, or personal optimism. There's a sure-fire test for that. It's a simple pulse check. When he's done with me, I'll be in a box or an urn.

Some geographical arrangements give us a laugh about this kind of thing every now and then. Our church campus is located right next door to the North Charleston chapel of a locally owned family mortuary, crematorium, and funeral service. We share parking lots with them and often collaborate at several levels. I always tell the staff my prayer for death is to find me dead in my desk chair so they can just roll me across the parking lot to the funeral directors next door. Gallows humor at its best.

God isn't through with us until we're dead. I've known ministers at every level of Christian service becoming immobilized by critical health issues, family circumstances, or other changes in their personal situation, including being asked to leave a church ministry situation. In more instances than I can

115

mention, many of them have adjusted their calling in ministry to suit the new parameters of their life, even if often short-term. A friend is a chaplain in a resort campground. Another serves with a volunteer fire department, while another rides with a sheriff's deputy. Many serve as hospital chaplains, volunteers, rescue mission cooks, or theme park counselors. One of the most attractive possibilities is to become a kingdom coach, like my friend Curt Bradford, or a convener of accountability groups. For most of us, there are next chapters in ministry, a time to step away from the rigors of our first calling and submit to His leadership in a ministry more suited to our circumstances. For me, that's what retirement is about, the next chapter.

One of my personal reasons is the conviction that our church needs fresh eyes. No fuddy-duddy, I'm comfortable with social media, digital technology, and new expressions of worship. My mind, however young, is wrapped in a sixty-five-year-old body with sixty-five-year-old sight, sound, smell, taste, and touch, and conditioning by sixty-five years of *Happy Days*. Try as I might, my instincts have reached the limit of their cultural accommodation. So every once in a while, I'll talk about broken records, a slow boat to China, the Peanut Gallery, and another day older and deeper in debt. The nine-thirty congregation smiles in acknowledgement. The eleven o'clock group scratches their heads, clueless as Fibber McGee. My basic orientation, in spite of my Nook, iPad, iPhone 6, MacBook, Bluetooth, Wi-Fi, Facebook, Twitter, Black Kia Soul, and Keurig coffee maker is still Pinky Lee and Humpty Dumpty—Baby Boomer all the way. So I'm convicted I need to let the next gen step up and lead our church to greater effectiveness in reaching the young community around us.

This is reality-bite time for us boomers. Many of us plan to stay active because we think we're the masters of navigating cultural change. Under that delusion, we believe we are the fresh mind, eyes, and heart that can bridge the generation gaps to more effectively reach millennials. Some of us can, but only a few. The church I've been honored to serve for eleven years is in a vibrant, youthful suburb, close to a growing university, a very nice shopping mall, and commercial growth. Lately I've learned that I'm not as cool as I think. Many of my friends are learning that skinny jeans, plaid shirts, and funky hair-dos aren't the stuff of cultural savvy. For me, it was just time to move aside so someone more acclimated to this fast world could guide the church through these treacherous waters.

But it's not an early out. The great majority of the ministers leaving His service every month aren't retirees or people experiencing health disabilities or other providential reasons for departing. No, the majority are just fed up with ministry. They're tired, worn, frustrated, and broken. And even though they may not admit it, whether or not God is finished with them seldom enters the equation. Mostly, they leave for a long list of emotional stresses, personal injuries, family pains, or just deep disappointments at the impact of church life on them and their families. Usually, the intense strains outweigh their senses of call. As a result, whether God is finished with them or not is a secondary consideration. Knowing that a man who doesn't adequately care for his family is worse than an unbeliever (1 Timothy 5:8) is enough for ministers to establish an entirely new set of priorities. Moving into a secular employment situation is often one of them.

Some pastors and staff ministers can't envision the joys of finishing because the joy of serving has been lost. The experts in human nature and the dynamics of work may still call it "burnout" because it certainly has some of earmarks of this classic psychological killer. But there's a difference, even if very subtle. Today many pastors, and churches for that matter, are in a funk, if you'll excuse the slang. It's a low-combustion malaise I usually refer to as "cave in," a sense of futility about ministry service. These servants become resigned to the realities of contemporary life and the loss of energy and effect in a vast number of congregations. Underneath our blockbuster, change-the-world façade is a cynicism about whether or not the civilization can actually be changed without cataclysmic events. We used to talk about the world going to you-know-where in a handbasket. Today, a great many pastors and kingdom servants believe we're already there and, with a shrug, deeply question whether the church in its current state of impotency can do very much about it.

It's another dimension of quitting, stepping away from God's vision and mission for the church and assuming the role of church caretaker. It's basically the kind of ministry departure the prophet Malachi wrote regarding Israel's priests. He wrote,

> Your words against me are harsh, says the Lord. Yet, you ask: How have we spoken against you. You have said, It is useless to serve God. What have we gained by keeping His requirements and walking mournfully before the Lord of Hosts?
> —Malachi 3:14

A while back, I met with a middle-aged pastor and his wife over lunch. They had been at their current church for thirteen years and were bored. He actually said he had retired five years earlier but hadn't informed the church to date. His wife said he didn't need to tell them; they already knew. He had taken early retirement but hadn't filed any papers. It was the retirement of futility, the malaise of misplaced mission. He had become resigned to a life of little impact and influence.

Over all of these subcategories of quitting, there's Romans 11:29. It's a stab in the heart for ministers who think their failures in one situation, resignations under fire, or troubles in the church invalidate their calls from God. There are certainly behaviors that can disqualify us for service, either temporarily or permanently. At the same time, most of us experience many uncertain hours, plenty of mistakes, judgment errors, and relational malfunctions to make us question our calls at times. His call, however, is bigger than even our worst miscalculations. Thinking He's finished with us because of some bonehead play is just ridiculous. When we think like that, we've made more of us and less of Him. Ask John the Baptist about that one!

Like Paul's reminder to Israel in God's great redemptive plan, "God's gracious gifts and calling are irrevocable." The Abrahamic covenant is eternal, and Israel will figure in the final accounting of all things. In like manner, His gifting and calling to ministry service are considered to be "without repentance" (as 11:29 reads in the KJV). This means He isn't finished with us until He's finished with us. Like most of our spiritual quests, our call to serve is mediated by Him and not us. We're not qualified to determine either its beginning or end. So in retirement or any other circumstance that may interrupt our kingdom service, He isn't finished with us until we're horizontal.

Finishing on Schedule

Jesus was keenly aware of a calibrated measure in the Father's redemptive plan. Even though His death was veiled until very specific announcements to the Twelve, there were numerous references to an appointed time or hour that were uniquely His. Even before He told them about a cross in Jerusalem, He spoke of completing God's work on earth. Early on he said, "My food is to do the will of Him who sent Me and to finish His work" (John 4:34). Clearly, there was a time element and a finish line evident in His daily regimen. Note the Scriptural references:

But when the completion of time came, God sent His Son, born of a woman, born under the law, to redeem those under the law, so that we might receive adoption as sons.

—Galatians 4:4–5

"Go into the city to a certain man," He said, "and tell him, 'The Teacher says, My time is near."

—Matthew 26:18

Then He came to the disciples and said to them, "Are you still sleeping and resting? Look, the time is near."

—Matthew 26:45, Mark 14:41

The time is fulfilled and the Kingdom of God has come near.

—Mark 1:15

Jesus told them, "My time has not yet arrived but your time is always at hand."

—John 7:6

"Go up to the festival yourselves. I'm not going up to the festival yet because My time has not yet fully come."

—John 7:8

"What has this concern of yours to do with Me woman?" asked Jesus. "My hour has not yet come."

—John 2:4

Then they tried to seize Him. Yet no one laid a hand on Him because His hour had not yet come.

—John 7:30

He spoke these words by the treasury, while teaching in the temple complex. But no one seized Him because His hour had not yet come.

—John 8:20

Jesus replied to them, "The hour has come for the Son of Man to be glorified."

—John 12:23

"Now My soul is troubled. What should I say—Father, save me from this hour? But that is why I came to this hour."

—John 12:27

Before the Passover Festival, Jesus knew that His hour had come to depart from this world to the Father.

—John 13:1

Jesus spoke these things, looked up to heaven, and said, "Father, the hour has come."

—John 17:1

For there is one God and one mediator between God and humanity, Christ Jesus, Himself human, who gave Himself-a ransom for all, a testimony at the proper time.

—1 Timothy 2:5–6

What is more, there were times that threatened the completion of His hour or appointed time. After the feeding of the five thousand, John wrote, "When the people saw the sign He had done, they said, 'This really is the Prophet who was to come into the world.' Therefore, when Jesus knew that they intended to make Him king, He withdrew to the mountain by Himself" (John 6:14–15). He demonstrated an awareness of a time for His finish.

A short time later, John added an almost parenthetical note: "After this, Jesus traveled to Galilee since He did not want to travel in Judea because the Jews were trying to kill Him" (John 7:1). In John's Gospel, there were several other notes about the plots to kill Him and fast-forward His death. Yet He continued to maneuver His entourage around those people who were trying to end His life so that He could attain that appointed hour or time.

All these textual references amplify His declaration from the cross, "It is finished" (John 19:30). His work, which was the will of the Father, was finished. It happened according to a heavenly timetable that governed His movements, His relationship to the multitudes, and His interaction with His opponents. Even more, there was also a determined sequencing of His activities that ensured the completion of this redeeming assignment.

It was characteristic of Jesus to finish. Over and over, Matthew's text chronicles the way He finished what He was doing while training the apostles and teaching the people. He finished a sermon (7:28), He finished giving orders (11:1), and He finished teaching specified parables (13:33) giving instructions (19:1), and saying certain things (26:1). Before He proclaimed, "It is finished," from the cross, John reminds us, "Jesus knew that everything was now accomplished that the Scripture might be fulfilled, He said, "I'm thirsty" (John 19:28).

Finishing was one of the character traits Jesus was building into His disciples. He talked to them often about the more pragmatic matters of kingdom service, including the endurance to see the work to the end. He taught His disciples to count the cost, build on a strong foundation, and complete the assignment given to them. What is more, He showed them the grace of going the distance.

And He is attempting to build that same attribute in us, the people to whom He has entrusted this Great Commission. He taught them about the rigors of serving, the troubles to be expected in the world. Additionally He modeled five disciplines to give them daily perspective for the journey. He spoke to them and graciously showed them the character traits of those who go to the end—endurance, intent, singleness of mission, humility, leadership, perspective, discernment, and refreshment. In every possible way, He emphasized the heart necessary to complete the task.

Five Promises for the Finish Line

Jesus is developing His character in me. Over the years, He has used two primary images to illustrate how this shaping occurs. One is the potter's wheel; the other is the smith's anvil. There have been times when He's lovingly placed His hands on my life to repair a marred spot or reshape something in me that had been dented, scraped, or damaged. This happens when I am soft clay in His hands. In other situations, I've been hard and fixed, stubborn to a fault. In these circumstances, He throws me on the anvil of His correction and discipline and pounds something into me.

One particular anvil time is memorable. It occurred when Harriet and I finally said yes to what we thought was His call to ministry. After we announced our decision to the people at work and church and to the community and our social circle, my first reaction was anger. I know that sounds harsh, and it was immature, I'll admit. But one morning, my mind flashed back to 1969, my sophomore year at the Citadel and a still, small voice I thought I heard calling me to His service. Then there were the words my mother spoke to Harriet in 1972. Suddenly, on the heels of what really was a very sweet and encouraging time, I was angry. Why had God waited so long to clarify His claim on us? That week, we wrestled with an issue that troubles many of us. Basically, I was angry with God because I thought we had wasted ten years of our lives. It was an occasion that could have finished me before I started. Once again, it was one of those times when I had increased and had allowed Him to decrease in me.

Rather than letting this root of bitterness grow deeper, we went to the Word and learned a few things about the kingdom. In the process, He taught the accountant in me lessons about the economy of heaven. With five Bible verses, He taught us that there is no waste in His economy and that only His work in us can thrust us through the rigors of serving Him. So the five lessons and verses are

Lesson One: God is always working.

> But Jesus responded to them, My Father is still working, and I am working also.
>
> —John 5:17

I memorized this verse in the NIV many years ago. It reads, "My Father is always at His work, and I too am working, to this very hour" (John 5:17, NIV). If He is always working, then there is no waste. This one verse dissipated the anger that bubbled to the surface in the days right after we answered His call. It was a thrilling discovery. God would use all of my previous church, family, and work experience in shaping me for the pastorate. What a blessing.

God will use even our darkest hours of ministry service too. If you're in the aftermath of disappointment or momentary failure, remember His economic principles. He isn't finished with you yet!

Lesson Two: God is always working for my good.

We know that all things work together for the good of those who love God: those who are called according to His purpose.

—Romans 8:28

Once again, it sounds so elementary and basic, that He is always working for our good. In times of pain and suffering, it's hard to see the good or even detect it. We are so distracted by the immediacy of our pain that we cannot imagine the good He may have in it.

But as C.S. Lewis wrote, "Pain insists upon being attended to. God whispers to us in our pleasures, speaks in our consciences, but shouts in our pains. It is His megaphone to rouse a deaf world."[6] It is in our most terrible hours that we are most apt to hear His voice.

Just as clearly, we have to know that this promise doesn't mean that everything will be good. The church circumstances that have led many of us to the point of quitting cannot be classified as good by any stretch of the imagination or positive spin. His promise is more redemptive in nature. He uses even our worst circumstances to shape it for our good.

There was an occasion when a dear friend was presented to a local congregation to be their new pastor. When the congregational vote was tallied, he received less than the percentage mandated by their bylaws. He and his family were crushed. Later, he was chosen as pastor of a truly needy congregation. He led them for more than twenty-five years. It is one of the most thrilling church turnaround stories in the history of Southern Baptists.

Lesson Three: God is working His purpose in my life.

> *For it is God who is working in you, enabling you both to will and to act for his good purpose.*
>
> —*Philippians 2:13*

This may be the hardest lesson of all. He is working to fulfill His purpose in us, and not our own. How often do we dream and plan our kingdom service as if it were just another career tract. Sure, we have goals and ambitions, like every other human being. The step down, the step of humility, should occur at the front of our Christian experience and continue in our calling from Him. Still, we know our strengths and gifts and would like to serve in the greatest kingdom capacity.

But He's not serving our purpose, but His. His work in us, and through us, is for His purpose and not ours. We must learn this soon.

Lesson Four: God will complete what He has started in me.

> *I am sure of this, that He who started a good work in you will carry it on to completion until the day of Christ Jesus.*
>
> —*Philippians 1:6*

The other day I posted this verse on Twitter with the note, "If you are contemplating quitting your ministry today, please read

Philippians 1:6," I got eleven contacts within fifteen minutes. I don't remember if it was a Monday, but perhaps so. Maybe that's why there were so many immediate hits.

Every day, this is a two-by-four upside the head. He started this ministry journey, and He must finish it, according to His promise. When we walk away, unless at His clear and obvious prodding, we are short-circuiting the work that only He can do.

Honestly, retirement was against the grain for me. I loved being a pastor, could not imagine any other calling in my life, and had already decided to remain in the pastoral role till death. Then there was the leading, the deep impression that He had something better for me as a last chapter. So, actually, He finished this work as He promised. Like the calling, I fought Him all the way.

Lesson Five: God works in me so that people will stand in awe of Him.

> *I know that all God does will last forever; there is no adding to it or taking from it. God works so that people will be in awe of Him.*
> —*Ecclesiastes 3:14*

This was another bombshell for me—that when He finishes what He started in me, He will be honored for what He's accomplished and not me. He doesn't call us so that people can talk about what great men or women we are or what great things we'll accomplish. Even at the finish, it's not about people commiserating with us, putting their arms around us, understanding why we're stepping away, or telling us the good things we need to hear. They'll talk about His faithfulness in finishing what He started.

Here's an Instant Message from God

The finish line should always be in sight because He keeps it there. He started this work in us, and He will bring it to completion. Continuation isn't primarily about our resolve, resourcefulness, or resiliency. As sharp and as on point as so many of us truly are, there will be times when our life circumstances, as well as certain crises at church, will be bigger than us. According to these five promises, they will never overshadow Him or interrupt the work He is doing in us. When it's done, people won't be raving about the great job we've done. They'll be in awe of Him.

It's nothing new, this absolute dependence on Him. Recently, however, it's as if a subtle veneer of humanism has overlaid our concept of calling. Perhaps this is why the writer of Hebrews told us to keep our eyes on Jesus, the author and finisher of our faith. Evidently the hard stuff of serving Him tends to shift our attention away from Him and to our unfulfilled personal dreams and aspirations, the many hurts and injuries of church service, the weight of family stress, and the elusive markers of success that seem so out of reach for so many of us. As a result, many of us walk away under the storm clouds of failure, disappointment, or disillusionment.

A few months ago a young pastor dropped by my office unannounced. His church was forty or fifty miles up the road. That morning, frustrated and stymied after another long, contentious deacons meeting, he took his children to school and then started driving. When he realized he was a couple of blocks from our church, he turned in. So we did what I usually do: we went to Starbucks for a cup of Komodo Dragon.

When we were seated he said, "I'm done!" I usually play it clueless, so I replied, "Done with what?" That's all it took. His rant lasted for a good ten minutes, most of it about what he could no longer do, all the church drama that confounded and disarmed him, and a catalog of his own personal failures and inadequacies. I listened patiently, which is usually a real test for me. He finally asked, "What should I do?"

I told him to have another cup of coffee and asked what the rest of his day looked like. He had arranged for his wife to pick the children up from school and was free for the remainder of the day. So we went to one of my places, Summerall Chapel at the Citadel. It's a historic place, the flags of the fifty states displayed around the worship space, plaques in memory of graduates killed in action, and markers of historic significance. I told him this was where I learned that I could not measure up on my own.

Sitting in a pew, I asked him what his being done had to do with anything. For forty-five minutes, I walked him through the thought processes I've tried to relate in this book. After lunch, he went home and is still serving at that same church. Later that week, I received a note from him. Two words were written on the inner page: "Thank you." When we talked several weeks later, he thanked me for changing the ministry scorecard for him. It was the simple truth that Someone else is working in us and has promised to finish what He started.

Our leadership development strategies must take a U-turn. In the process of training individuals for kingdom service, we must emphasize the nature and permanence of God's calling, the character traits He seeks to develop in the people He calls, and the centrality of His work in us for the completion of that call. Those raised up for kingdom service should learn the disciplines modeled by Jesus to endure the hardships of servant leadership. Even more, we must realign our understanding of this high calling to Scripture and remember some of the elemental lessons that frame His call to us.

There is a gentle reminder of how this all started in the first place. Jesus told his disciples, "You did not choose Me, but I chose you" (John 15:16). His gracious call to kingdom service is an honor extended to those He selected. We cannot understand His choosing or the rationale that could ever make even one of us qualified to serve Him. And that's a problem contributing to the high dropout rate, the high self-expectation that easily distracts a group of overachievers. As we counsel, mentor, coach, and train those seeking to answer this call, we must resist pushing the ego buttons that produce self-reliant and independent ministers. The words "servant" and "superstar" just don't resonate.

Finishing the race or the course was a key illustration in Paul's epistles. He wrote, "I have fought the good fight, I have finished the race, I have kept the faith" (1 Timothy 4:7). Interestingly, he equated fighting the good fight and finishing the race with keeping the faith. In the first letter to the Corinthians, he offered another angle. He wrote,

> Don't you know that the runners in a stadium all race, but only one receives the prize? Run in such a way to win the prize. Now everyone who competes exercises self-control in everything. However, they do it to receive a crown that will fade away, but we have a crown that will never fade away. Therefore, I do not run like one who runs aimlessly or box-like one beating the air. Instead, I discipline my body and bring it under control, so that after preaching to others, I myself will not be disqualified.
> —1 Corinthians 9:24–25

The athletic motif certainly communicates spiritual truth because it typically underscores disciplines significant to spiritual leadership, albeit with less secular connotations.

Finishing, however, is the backdrop of Paul's references to the race. More importantly, possessing the right stuff for finishing is the meat—self-control and discipline as opposed to aimless running or beating the air. The race alluded to is clearly a distance competition rather than a sprint. The important thing is to finish. So the rigorous training and imposition of such strong physical stamina produces the traits necessary to finish.

In this particular text, there may be hints of sexual distractions. Paul doesn't want to be disqualified before he finishes the race. In that context, the discipline and self-control must have been critical avoidance measures to ensure he wouldn't be disqualified before the finish line. Even beyond erotic warnings, this instruction is equally useful when considering any of the dangers that could end participation in the race prematurely. The final lesson is powerful: Paul desired to live his personal life equal to the standards he had outlined in his preaching. To do so and finish the race, he learned discipline and self-control. Finishing, though, was the deal.

The world is turning that way today, making the disconnect of the church from culture seem even more pronounced. Being in the world stretches us to resist the values that may be claiming so many of our dear pastors every month. Society around us values getting in the race. To join up, sign up, enlist, or begin are the coinage in a culture of engagement. Being "all in," the language of the gaming table, is the buzz. But finishing is downplayed, whispered conversations between the builder generation, who knew about company men and marriages for life, and boomers who wished they had experienced a little more stability. To stay with something, and that would be just about anything, is foreign to the times.

It's a changing scorecard thing again. Valuing the start over the finish is a societal inversion that touches the contemporary church in many ways. One is evident in the local church. Today, church roles are perhaps more fluid than ever, people jumping on board, expecting something magical for their children, marriages, addictions, counseling needs, relationships, and all the other affinities. The front doors of growing churches are spinning off their revolving mechanisms. Great music, high-tech electronics, social media networks, innovative preaching, ministry specialties for every need, children and youth pizzazz, all have the church rocking off its foundation. At the same time, the proverbial back door is now an off-ramp where the disappointed exit. They didn't get what they expected so they moved on to the folks down the street.

Spiritual calling may be a second area of concern. That so many leave the ministry every month may be indicative of more than just the hard elements of serving Him. There's another possibility that must be considered if the scorecard is to be changed. Follow this: Seminary enrollment is at an all-time high. Fewer and fewer of them are indicating calls to traditional pastoral ministry, however. Most are preparing for church planting or replanting, teaching, nontraditional missions, para-church ministry, or missionary assignments. Most have a sense of God's call but no specific guidance or direction. Many are there to receive religious instruction and listen to God for clarification. Beyond something more specific, they are the generation that wants to (1) change the world, (2) help other people, (3) make a difference, (4) work in exotic areas, (5) solve cultural ills, like racism, poverty, inequality, or spiritual error, (6) pioneer new work, (7) activate collegiate ministries, (8) form cross-cultural alliances, (9) spearhead adoption and fostering programs, or (10) get into all the places churches have been excluded, and hundreds of other worthy reasons. Without clear definition, many turn to opportunities in local churches. When the local traditional church doesn't satisfy their inner stirrings, the result is to quit.

Reversing entrenched systems is difficult is nonhierarchical denominations with basically autonomous, independent congregations. In Southern Baptist life, there isn't one scorecard; there are forty-five thousand, the number of our congregations. The local church is the basic filter for people entering the ministry. Ordination is a local church prerogative. Applicants to attend any of our six seminaries must be recommended by a local congregation. Associational and state convention groups serve churches by assisting them in these important processes.

What is more, young people are encouraged, perhaps even pushed, toward ministry careers and the paths that lead them there. It is one big glory, hallelujah time when someone expresses interest in pursuing a call into ministry. There are business conferences, church votes, slaps on the back, covered-dish dinners, ordination committees, scholarships, and rituals particular to every church to drive and facilitate the process. Even the ordination committees, feared by applicants in the past, usually involve soft questioning and gentle correction when an answer veers off the denominational line. There is little in the process to question or clarify the call or further define the specifics of the applicants aim. It's all about beginning.

To reduce the number of people leaving the ministry will require downplaying the start and emphasizing the finish. It's a topic we don't talk about all that much, the many joys of the crown of righteousness; hearing Him say well done, good and faithful slave; entering the rest promised to the obedient; being complete and mature. Seldom do we cover a discouraged, broken pastor or minster with the many biblical words about the one who's standing at the finish line, the one who started this thing and will finish it. There's little in the system, beyond occasional appreciation days and anniversaries, to focus on completing what was started. The call then to "Finish. Period." must be a marker that is announced and celebrated in every church and denominational structure.

My hardest challenge before ministry was to finish knob year at the Citadel. It's like military boot camp with a nine-month duration. Entering from high school, I was overweight, soft, and totally out of shape. The physical demands pushed me to my personal limits every day. Physical training involved obstacle courses, long distance running, hundreds of push-ups, and climbing that infernal rope. In addition, there was a good bit of verbal abuse as well, so there were layers of emotional strain added to the physical tests. But they fast-forwarded us to the finish line every day too. Every day, while most of us were on the verge of quitting, a senior cadet would show us his ring. It was the prize we all sought, the carrot on a stick they kept in front of us every single day so we wouldn't just walk away. It took us to the finish line. In our four years as Citadel cadets, the rituals of graduation were visible and obvious in everything we did. The system focused us on finishing. Since 1842, it was one of the ways they kept underclassmen enrolled in a rugged system that we had to pay for. We fantasized about wearing that ring and standing in the long, gray line of graduation, a line stretching back to 1842.

Colleges do that kind of thing well. They have team mascots and colors, theme songs, alma maters, alumni associations, personalized bricks on the alumni road, and hundreds of ways to reduce attrition rates while students are still in school and to keep their graduates connected. Corporate America has training programs, career development counselors, retirement systems, parking privileges, and many other ways to cultivate, prepare, and keep their leaders. Surely, God's people can make the conversation about finishing too.

Just say. Finish. Period.

Just say. Finish. Period.

Just say. Finish. Period.

Finish. Period. Finish. Period. Finish. Period. Finish. Period. Finish. Period. Finish. Period. Finish. Period. Finish. Period. Finish. Period. Finish. Period. Finish. Period. Finish. Period. Finish. Period. Finish. Period. Finish. Period. Finish. Period. Finish. Period. Finish. Period. Finish. Period. Finish. Period.

So Then, Finish. Period.

So the last chapter is what? A conclusion? Afterthoughts? A summary? In this context, about the only things that works for me is so then, Finish. Period. Conclusion could work as a final chapter only if there was an actual conclusion in the final paragraphs. In this book, there's a stack of conclusions, and if there was one in the last few sentences, it would be conclusion number something or other.

"Afterthoughts" as a last chapter title doesn't really fit the occasion either. They would be things I should have written earlier but didn't remember to include. Afterthoughts would work if they were actually BTW ideas, what came to me after I had written all I know. They would be the "oh, yeah" stuff.

Then, again, a summary isn't a very appropriate descriptive if you want people to read the rest. If it's a good, accurate summary, readers could fast forward to the final pages and have little need to give attention to what came before.

This one will be, with little fanfare, "So Then, Finish. Period." It's just a way to put a wrap on the project, the "–30–" to mark the end. For me and, I pray, a majority of readers, these final thoughts will be more of a to-do list, projected actions that may help stem the mass exodus from church service. It will not actually define or establish the finish, but will remind us there is one, and then point us in that direction.

Yes, there's the journey. In ministry, it begins with a call from God. Mine involved a sense of His call to ministry at age nineteen, after my sophomore year at the Citadel, and ten years of trying to ignore it. Through two concluding years of college, six years with a large commercial bank, and two years of hospital financial administration, I couldn't shake the deep impression that He was calling me to pastoral ministry. When that call was clarified, it was without doubt the most thrilling and liberating moment of our lives. Harriet, Liz, Brian, and I liquidated our comfortable life to enter seminary. Shortly thereafter, we were called to Woodland Baptist Church as pastor. The day they ordained me, June 1, 1980, is among the greatest days of my life. It was a central milestone in what has been an emotion packed journey. It was the start.

After my call to Woodland Baptist Church, the very next day in fact, reality set in. I was asked to perform my first funeral, an unbeliever who lived in the community. A church member was diagnosed with cancer that same week. For the first time, I was on the preparation treadmill. Shut-ins needed visiting, there was my first deacons meeting, and we moved into the parsonage. The glitter of ordination was overshadowed by a busy, enthusiastic church. They were great, in every way kind, patient, compassionate, and supportive. But the to-do list of a full-time student, pastor, husband, and father meant long days, late nights, and frayed nerves. Nobody had bothered to warn me about the frayed nerves part.

That's when Dr. Carroll Trotter, professor of preaching at Southeastern Baptist Theological Seminary, had prayer meeting with me. Now, he and I had some significant theological differences that we both acknowledged and appreciated. But that day he lectured me about the rigors of ministry. He encouraged me, in my first months of pastoral service, to take certain, definitive steps to ensure longevity in ministry. Back then, he referred to burnout, the popular buzzword of that age for expending our physical, emotional, and spiritual fuel too quickly. His were wise words. They have been in the backdrop of personal ministry for thirty-four years. Months later, I had that Binkley Chapel pity party and hyperlearning session mentioned in the introduction. His counsel and the learning grid I climbed in the chapel were crucial in setting a pace for the years of service ahead.

You don't hear too much about burnout these days. The extremes of our times reflect stronger language and more tragic outcomes. Today, people just quit or, worse, commit suicide. We all know that flight is the most common response in dealing with any kind of conflict. Running away is an instinctive action. Even more, in ministry, ordained people experience a serious sense of failure when ministry goals and vision lag behind all the human expectations. Failing God is an emotional and spiritual black hole that quickly engulfs us. Still, even escape is symptomatic. Prevention requires more definitive steps and a clear understanding of His call to persevere to the end.

The four congregations He called me to serve blessed us beyond our expectations. Each was a church in transition of one sort or another. Woodland had to envision and prepare for the urban sprawl of the Research Triangle—Raleigh, Durham, and Chapel Hill, North Carolina. First Baptist Church of Goose Creek (South Carolina) left her rural organizational moorings to more fully reach a vast, quickly growing suburban community. Hampton Heights Baptist Church (Greenville, South Carolina) was recovering from a church split and several years of stagnancy. Northwood Baptist Church was seeking new renewed vision after the retirement of their pastor of twenty-seven years.

Each of them anticipated change. This meant they needed leadership, vision, and a strong work ethic. More than anything else, each of them needed a pastor and staff who were in it for the duration. Conflict was inevitable in such vibrant and opportune mission fields. Longevity enabled us to guide the ministries of the church through consistent vision casting and strong credibility. All too often, these traits of spiritual leadership are subsumed in the wake of rapid turnover and ministry movement. To recapture a place at the table of ideas, God's people and His churches must resist the lockstep of a secular culture and incorporate the steps of Christ into our personal practice of ministry.

So what's the final to-do list? How can we change the scorecards that are leading us through such a treacherous time?

(1) Before you quit, read the five promises for the finish line in chapter 6.

(2) Every one of you, write the epoch of your calling in several paragraphs and read it every day.

(3) Frame your ministry, life, and passion verses. Mount them on a prominent wall in your home or office so you can read them every day. If you don't have these verses selected, then ask God to show them to you as a means of directing your kingdom service.

(4) Encourage someone in the ministry. Ask colleagues how they're doing. Go beyond the surface with them. Push them for honesty. Then talk about the joys.

(5) Practice the five steps regularly—down, up, back, aside, away. Find a place and a time to experience each.

(6) Make a list of the character traits you think He is developing in you. Ask Him specifically for those you

find in short supply. Remember: you have not because you ask not.

(7) Fix your eyes on the One who started this work in you, the same One who will finish it.

That's the deal, isn't it? He must be our model. There's no other way. He practiced these five steps and is developing His character in each of us. The final instruction, then, is to follow them, and Finish. Period.

ὁ λέγων ἐν αὐτῷ μένειν ὀφείλει, καθὼς ἐκεῖνος περιεπάτησε, καὶ αὐτὸς οὕτω περιπατεῖν.

Look it up—1 John 2:6

Notes

Introduction

[1]   Lane, Bo, 2014. http://www.expastors.com. A website created and maintained by Bo Lane, with facts and statistics about pastoral or ministerial tenure and up-to-date articles by informed contributors. Accessed many times from May 2014 through November 2014.

[2]   Ibid. The primary question posed at the http://expastors.com website is "Why Do So Many Pastor's Leave the Ministry?"

[3]   Expastors.com research indicates that seventeen hundred pastors leave the ministry every month. This number has been re-visited by many research institutions. More recent work indicates a lower number, estimated at closer to 250 per month.

[4]   IntoThyWord.org is a Bible study website affiliated with the Francis A. Schaeffer Institute for Christian Leadership Development. The primary contributor is Dr. Richard J. Krejcir, nephew of Dr. Schaeffer. This site was accessed many times from May 2014 through November 2014.

[5]   Peacemaker Ministries is dedicated to resolving personal and corporate conflict through the application of biblical principles. Ken Sande is the president of the ministry. Their research on pastoral tenure is available at www.peacemaker.net. This site has been studied on many occasions since January 2001 in reference to church and personal conflict.

[6]   "Be Thou My Vision" was translated from old Irish into English in 1909. Hope Publishing Company holds a copyright on the tune "Slane" since 1989. The words are in the public domain. The words quoted in this text are from the Baptist Hymnal, Nashville, Sunday School Board of the Southern Baptist Convention, 1975.

7   Ibid.
8   Charleston Post and Courier (SC), articles and pictures from April 5, 2014.

Chapter 1

1   William Barclay, The Master's Men. Phoenix, AZ: Phoenix Press, 1985.
2   Thom Rainer, "Ten Traits of Pastors Who Have Healthy Long-term Tenure," *Thom S. Rainer Blog*, September 29, 2014. Accessed many times between May 2014 and November 2014.

Chapter 2

1   Reggie McNeal, *Get a Life: It Is All about You.* Nashville: B and H Publishing Group, 2007.
2   Thom Rainer, "The Dangerous Third Year of Pastoral Tenure," *Thom S. Rainer Blog*, June 18, 2014. Accessed many times between May 2014 and November 2014.
3   http://www.expastors.com, accessed many times between May 2014 and November 2014.
4   Henry Blackaby and Richard Blackaby, *Spiritual Leadership: Moving People on to God's Agenda*. Nashville: B and H Books, 2001.
5   Leonard Bernstein, quoted in many sources but used here from Quoteland.com, accessed many times between May 2014 and November 2014.
6   Jack Wellman, "Why Are We Losing So Many Churches in the United States?" http://patheos.com, accessed many times between May 2014 and November 2014 but quoted from an article published October 26, 2013.
7   Warnall Road Baptist Church, Kansas City, Missouri, John Mark Clifton, Pastor.
8   Ken Sande, *The Peacemaker*. Grand Rapids, Baker Books: 2004.

Chapter 3

1   Behindthebooks.ivpress.com, a blog published by Intervarsity Press, "How Many New Christian Books Are There?" by Al Hsu, May 11, 2007.

2   http://www.pewforum.org, the Pew Research Religion and Life Project, "Nones on the Rise," October 9, 2012. Accessed on many occasions between May 2014 and November 2014.

3   Ed Stetzer, "Mission Trends: Four Trends for Churches to Consider," *The Exchange*, A Blog by Ed Stetzer *Christianity Today*, June 2, 2014.

4   E. Glenn Wagner, *Escape from Church, Inc.* Grand Rapids: Zondervan, 1999.

5   John Dickson, *Humilitas: A Lost Key to Life, Love, and Leadership.* Grand Rapids: Zondervan, 2011.

6   Jim Collins, *Good to Great.* New York: Harper Collins, 2001.

7   Tom Rath and Barry Conchie, *Strength Based Leadership.* New York: Gallup Press, 2008.

8   Henry Blackaby and Richard Blackaby, *Spiritual Leadership: Moving People on to God's Agenda*, Nashville: B and H Books, 2001.

9   Ibid.

10 Tom Rath, *Strengths Finder 2.0.* New York: Gallup Press, 2007.

11 Malcolm Gladwell, *The Tipping Point.* Boston: Little, Brown, and Company, 2002.

12 C. S. Lewis, *The Silver Chair (The Chronicles of Narnia).* New York, Harper-Collins Trophy Edition, 2000. As quoted by http://goodreads.com, accessed many times from May 2014 through November 2014.

13 Jason Jennings and Laurence Haughton, It's Not the Big that Eat the Small, But the Fast that Eat the Slow. New York: Harper Collins, 2002.

14 Henry Blackaby and Richard Blackaby, *Spiritual Leadership: Moving People on to God's Agenda*. Nashville: B and H Books, 2001.

15 L. D. Johnson, *The Morning after Death.* Macon, GA: Smythe Helwys Publishing, 2008.

16 Tom Rath, *Strengths Finder 2.0.* New York: Gallup Press, 2007.

Chapter 4

1   http://wikipedia.org/wiki/Quo_vadis, Wikipedia dictionary, Quo Vadis?, accessed several times between May 2014 and November 2014.

2   http://en.wikipedia.org/wiki/Church_of_Domine_Quo_Vadis, Wikipedia dictionary, Church of the Domine Quo Vadis, accessed several times between May 2014 and November 2014.

3   Strong's Greek Concordance, "4074. Petros," as revealed by BibleHub, http://biblehub.com/greek/4074, accessed many times between May 2014 and November 2014.

4   Strong's Greek Concordance, "2495. Ionas," as revealed by BibleHub, http://biblehub.com/greek/2495, accessed many times between May 2014 and November 2014.

Chapter 5

1   Henry Blackaby, *Experiencing God, Knowing and Doing the Will of God*. Nashville: B and H Books, 2008.

2   Ibid.

3   Henry Blackaby, *Experiencing God: Knowing and Doing the Will of God*, Nashville: B and H Books, 2008.

4   Winston Churchill, as quoted by the quotation site http://thinkexist.com/quotation/the_nose_of_the_bulldog_has_been_slanted/177150.html, accessed many times between May 2014 and November 2014.

5   Strong's Greek Concordance, "1401.Doulos" as revealed by BibleHub, http://biblehub.com/greek/1401, accessed many times between May 2014 and November 2014.

6   Richard N. Bolles, *How to Find Your Mission in Life*. Berkeley: Ten-Speed Press, 2005.

Chapter 6

1   Rick Warren, *The Purpose-Driven Life*. Grand Rapids: Zondervan: 2002.

2   Ibid.

3   Reggie McNeal, *Get a Life: It Is All about You*. Nashville: B and H Publishing, 2007.

4   Darlene Zschech, Israel Houghton, Kari Jobe. Victor's Crown. Integrity Praise Music/Sound of the New Breed/Worship Music/ EWI, 2013.

5   Thom Rainer, "What Happens When Boomer Pastors Retire." *Thomas S. Rainer* September 17, 2014.

6   C. S. Lewis, The Problem of Pain, as quoted in Goodreads, https:// www.goodreads.com/quotes/422142-we-can-ignore-even-pleasure but-pain-insists-upon-being, accessed many time between May 2014 and November 2014.

Bibliography

Barclay, William. *The Master's Men*. Phoenix: Phoenix Press, 1985.

Blackaby, Henry. *Experiencing God: Knowing and Doing the Will of God*. Nashville: B and H Books, 2008.

Blackaby, Henry, and Richard Blackaby. *Spiritual Leadership, Moving People on to God's Agenda*. Nashville: B&H Books, 2001.

Bolles, Richard. *How to Find Your Mission in Life*. Berkeley: Ten-Speed Press, 1991.

Cox, Harvey. *The Secular City*. New York City: MacMillan, 1965.

Collins, Jim. *Good to Great*. New York: Harper Collins Publishers, 2001.

Dickson, John. *Humilitas: A Lost Key to Life, Love, and Leadership*. Grand Rapids: Zondervan, 2011.

Gladwell, Malcolm. *The Tipping Point*. Boston: Little Brown and Company, 2001.

Jennings, Jason, and Laurence Haughton. *It's Not the Big That Eat the Small…It's the Fast That Eat the Slow*. New York: Harper Collins, 2002.

Johnson, L.D. *The Morning after Death*. Macon: Smythe Helwys Publishing, 2008.

McNeal, Reggie, *Get a Life: It is All About You*. Nashville: B and H Publishing, 2007.

Rath, Tom. *StengthsFinder 2.0*. New York: Gallup Press, 2007.

Rath, Tom and Barry Conchie. *Strengths Based Leadership*. New York: Gallup Press, 2008.

Sande, Ken. *The Peacemaker*. Grand Rapids: Baker Books, 2004.

Wagner, Glenn. *Escape from Church, Inc*. Grand Rapids: Zondervan, 1999.

About the Author

Sonny Holmes recently retired after thirty-four years of pastoral ministry. He and Harriet have been married for forty-two years. They are the parents of daughter Elizabeth, who married Scott Carpenter, and grandparents of John Lewis and Laura. Sonny studied business at the Citadel and has MDiv and DMin degrees from Southeastern Baptist Theological Seminary. He was president of the South Carolina Baptist Convention in 2011 and served terms as a trustee of Charleston Southern University and Southeastern Baptist Theological Seminary. In retirement, Sonny will support his website, finish.period.com, and provide coaching for ministers in areas of calling, leading, and finishing.

CPSIA information can be obtained at www.ICGtesting.com
Printed in the USA
LVOW06s2048151015

458440LV00002B/3/P